"Insanity is doing the same thing over and over again and expecting different results."

Albert Einstein

CAMPAIGN TO WIN

How You Can Use Communicating
Skills To Win Elections

BRENT NELSON PH. D.

The companion book *Campaign To Win 2, The Seminar and Workbook*, is based on a seminar that was developed for individuals, groups, and organizations about how to effectively communicate with the public. It applies to candidates running for office as well as individuals, businesses, and organizations who want to motivate people to take action like buying a product or voting for a candidate. It can be used as a seminar guidebook or with companion books *Campaign To Win 2, Capitol Hillary, Managing Uncertainty, or Be Smarter, Happier, Better-Looki*ng. Available on Amazon.

The author conducts a limited number of speaking engagements and seminars. He can be reached through his publisher at htrhill@yahoo.com.

HH

Heather Hill

Cover Art BNelson

Copyright © 2016 - All Rights Reserved

ISBN 10: 0692652094 - ISBN 13: 978-0692652091

Table of Contents

Preface

Albert Einstein was once quoted as saying, "Insanity is doing the same thing over and over again and expecting different results."

The way some candidates campaign it seems like they don't want to win. They use old-fashioned, out-dated ideas and failed ways that haven't worked for years, even decades.

So, why don't they change? Because they just don't get it.

The country has changed, the people have changed, the nature of campaigning has changed, yet they cling to their old ways and then wonder why they lose.

Campaign To Win explains how politicians can create a message that makes a connection with the people to gain their support and motivate them to vote for them. This is how they get people to volunteer, campaign, and give them money.

Campaign To Win provides insights about how candidates can communicate more effectively with the people to help them win. It can be used by practically any candidate running for virtually any office as a playbook to win.

This book is about how to create a message that makes a connection with voters to motivate them to support a candidate. It is not meant to change the substance of that message.

It is not about other aspects of campaigning like getting out the vote, fundraising, event planning, endorsements, branding, or organizing.

It is meant bring a campaign to the next level by adding a persuasive element that will enhance each of these.

The purpose of this book is to examine how candidates get people to support them. Not just why they vote for them, but also why they volunteer, give money, and form strong opinions of people they have never met and often know very little about.

This book examines not only the process by which elections are won and lost, but also how and why this process works. It is a process that can be utilized by practically any candidate running for virtually any office, so they can Campaign To Win.

Plan to Win

Chapter 1
Why Campaign To Lose

One of the most challenging problems in any governmental system is establishing the right to rule. In ancient times, rulers claimed descendancy from the gods or ruled by divine right.

Over time, the method of establishing the right to rule has changed, however, the need for leaders and governments to prove their ability to lead has changed little.

As kings and courts gave way to presidents and parliaments, the people had a more direct influence in the choice of their government through the elective process.

This established the notion of a government's claim to rule by popular mandate as being conferred directly by the people.

As civilization developed and changed, so did the nature of government. Few governments today refer to supernatural forces to support the political order, however, the fundamental principle remains the same.

This is the process of legitimation of political power. It is how a government and its leaders are invested with the right to rule, or govern society.

The absence of a clear mandate to lead can create confusion or even anarchy, which has resulted in the overthrow of political regimes through military coups or populist movements.

No less significant are the gains and losses of political influence by leaders in democratic governments that can affect their ability to govern. So, the process of political legitimation is more one of persuasive negotiation than a test of power or military might.

The legitimation of political power to establish an administration's right to govern can be characterized as the process by which a government and its leaders are invested with power by the members of a society.

The relationship between a society and its leaders is constantly changing. Both the government and individual politicians can be subject to this process gaining or losing legitimacy concurrently or separately.

A leader or administration is rarely perceived as having an absolute right to govern or having no right to govern at all. Instead, there is some intermediate degree of rightness and support inherent in each institution. For instance, Congress can suffer the loss of esteem while that of individual members can remain high.

The degree to which a leader is deemed to be legitimate to govern is determined by the number of citizens who accept the rule of the government.

Even after winning election to office, a president can suffer a loss of legitimacy that hampers their ability to govern or move legislation through Congress.

A government and its leaders have the ability, through use of political rhetoric to convince, condition, or alter the perceptions of the people as to their appropriateness to govern.

The degree of legitimacy in a government and its leaders can be seen as a function of their ability to foster the people's faith in a regime.

The adversarial nature of the American political system is likely to express itself in the loss of influence of the party that loses power and a significant increase in influence of the party that gains power.

The ability of a government to gain the people's support involves ongoing communication between a government's leaders and the people regarding the validation of mutual goals and needs based on reaffirming a shared set of values.

In order to legitimize their claim for office, candidates often draw upon forces recognized by the electorate. These forces can include traditions, values, beliefs, and mandates from the people.

In the United States, two political parties vie for the right to govern through popular election. In such a system, this regular change of power, while having become routine, presents subtle problems in the establishment of a candidate's legitimate right to govern.

In the democratic context, the process of legitimation is accomplished rhetorically.

An election campaign can be seen as a series of persuasive rhetorical attempts by both sides to undermine their opponent's legitimacy and their right to govern, while bolstering their own.

The Methodology to This Madness

Examining traditional campaign issues like a character, fitness for office, experience, the economy, approval ratings, and scandals seemed to add little insight into what makes a winner.

Focusing on the issues may not determine a candidate's success, but instead success may be more due to the persuasive characterization of popular issues.

The key factor in explaining what makes a winner may lie in how these characterizations are shared with the public to motivate their behavior.

The research for this book examined campaigns from a candidate's announcement to run to Election Day. It analyzed the issues raised by candidates and how they characterized them to the public.

It utilizes scholarly research for the purpose of reporting, commentary, analysis, and criticism to create new insights into public discourse.

The material utilized came from the candidates, their organizations, polls, and the media including speeches, advance texts, transcripts, press releases, campaign literature, books, television, news conferences, and appearances. This material was selected for its representativeness of these campaigns.

This book is not intended to advance a particular type of political discourse, policy, or ideology. It is intended as scholarly research for educational and critical analysis of the effectiveness of the use of dramatic narratives to share meaning to create and sustain social reality.

Poll data was utilized in new and creative ways to determine the effectiveness of how candidates share meaning with the voters. In evaluating shared meanings, several poll measures are utilized throughout the campaign.

One measure is a candidate's approval rating, which measures the percentage of the people who approve or disapprove of how they are doing their job.

Other poll measures include each candidate's favorability and unfavorability ratings. Potential voters are asked if they have a favorable or unfavorable opinion of a candidate giving them a favorable and unfavorable rating.

This information can be interpreted as a measure of a candidate's legitimacy and public perception of their right to govern.

People are also asked if the election is held today, which candidate would they vote for. They are then asked if their support is either strong or weak.

Specific issues were also measured to determine how important the public viewed them and how well they felt the candidates would handle them.

The extent that public opinion reflects a candidate's characterization of their persona or events tells how well voters are sharing meaning with their dramatic narratives and a particular version of social reality.

How the media reported and interpreted events is also examined to see how each candidate's view of social reality is being shared by them and the general public.

The Nature of Uncertainty

Life is chaotic. Things can happen unexpectedly or for no apparent reason. We want to know why things happen to us, so we look for answers.

We want to know what to expect from other people, so we try to understand their motivations. We want to know what will happen in the future, so we can make plans. Not knowing these things can create uncertainty.

Politics and government can be a source of public uncertainty. We want to know what to expect from our leaders. We want to know how the government will affect our lives, now and in the future.

When there is a low degree of uncertainty it creates stability. When we don't know what to expect, there can be a high degree of uncertainty creating apprehension and tension.

It can be beneficial to measure the degree of public uncertainty in many areas, such as with an uncertainty index, because it has the power to motivate people's behavior.

When people experience something unfamiliar to them it can create tension making them uncomfortable, which can motivate them to take action to reduce it.

This tension is often resolved through the construction of a social reality driven by the characterizations of real life events and experiences.

For instance, people want to know why the economy is bad and when it will improve, so they look for explanations. And they often look to politicians for those answers.

Many candidates reduce uncertainty about themselves and their policies by creating their own specialized version of social reality that not only explains their programs, but also includes a vision of what society should become.

Franklin Roosevelt had the New Deal, which created a vision of a renewed America being led out of the depression.

Dramatic narratives can also include heroes and villains and descriptions of their actions that can be characterized as good or bad.

How Shared Meaning Works

The process of sharing meaning deals with the human tendency to want to understand the motivation for people's behavior to reduce uncertainty about them.

The process of shared meaning is how a person makes a connection with other people, so that they see things in a similar way. This is how a candidate gains and maintains people's support.

Shared meaning can help to recall familiar stories for those who share them. If a specific story has not been shared, it would not make sense and the entire story would have to be explained.

So, when a candidate uses a shared meaning like conservative, liberal, tax and spend, or trickle down in a campaign, they do not have to retell the entire story. These shared meanings can be used to trigger positive qualities they have as well as negative characterizations about an opponent.

When people communicate, they talk about themselves often telling stories about their past experiences. When they do, they might edit these stories to make them more interesting and exciting to the listener.

When people understand and relate to these stories they share meaning. They have the same understanding of what they mean and possibly share their own stories about similar experiences.

This can create a connection, so they feel that they have something in common. This can make people seem more likable, even creating feelings of empathy.

Creating a Public Persona

Before entering the race for office, a candidate often develops a persona for public consumption, even if it is different from their actual personality. Their public persona often includes why they want to run, what they want to accomplish, what programs they would enact in office, and who they are and what they stand for as a candidate.

This book looks at three different types of candidates. It does not look at them in ideological terms like liberal, conservative or moderate. Nor does it look at them in party terms like Republican, Democrat, or independent.

Instead this book looks at three types of candidates in terms of their persona and experience. The incumbent who holds a public office and is running for re-election. Their opponent has likely been elected to other political offices, or they might be a newcomer with other political experience. They want to oust the incumbent from office.

Then there is the outsider, who is also a newcomer, but has little or no political experience. They have likely gained some public notoriety. They might have experience in business, the military, the media, or other field, which they use to claim legitimacy.

The evidence suggests that how these three types of candidates are characterized is more important to their electoral success than ideology, experience, or party affiliation.

A candidate's persona can be developed in the public eye, shaped by public opinion, and shared in the media over years of public service, as is often the case with an incumbent.

Candidates and their advisors may spend months or years developing a candidate's public persona in preparation for a campaign, as is common with the opponent.

A candidate's persona may develop spontaneously in public while being honed behind the scenes, evolving during the campaign. This usually happens with an outsider who may be a well-known personality or business person with little political experience.

Candidates create stories about themselves and their experiences to share meaning with the voters. They do this to make themselves appear more personable and likable so people will vote for them.

Dramatic Narratives

When people come together they often tell stories, but instead of giving an accounting of events, they may characterize and embellish what transpired. When people tell stories that have meaning to other people, they may join in and share their own similar experiences.

People share meaning by using dramatic narratives. These stories can be emotional and can motivate people to take action. When they share dramatic narratives, they have the same understanding of events and common ground is created.

Much of how we explain our experiences and understand reality is communicated through dramatic narratives.

Dramatic narratives consist of a story or the retelling of certain events. They often have an emotional and persuasive quality to make them more interesting or exciting. They are created to have a desired effect on people like informing, entertaining, or persuading them.

Dramatic narratives characterize events from a particular point of view. They are invested with meaning by the people who create and share them.

They are often given a dramatic, persuasive, or emotional quality to make them more interesting or dramatic. They characterize an event or person to give them meaning, so people can better understand them.

Dramatic narratives can characterize people and their behavior as acceptable or not, which tells people what values are important. This can create the perception of heroes and villains who exhibit behaviors that are good or evil.

A candidate might cast themselves in their own dramatic narratives as the hero who will save the people from a villain who is out to destroy everything the people hold dear.

Examining dramatic narratives provides a way to understand the shared meanings in what a person says, as well as their underlying motives. Shared meanings tell us about our culture, what we value, what we believe, and who we are.

Dramatic narratives are often action based to involve the public who must take action, along with the hero, to save them from a terrible fate if nothing is done. This action can be to support a cause, a politician or policy, donate money, or vote.

It can be said that literary forms fall into two basic categories, fact and fiction. There is the assumption that if someone is not telling the truth, they are lying.

If fact comprises those things that are verifiably true and fiction is an imaginative creation developed through invention that does not represent actual reality, then political candidates may do neither.

Instead, they take an inherent reality, like the economy or health care, choose a few pertinent items and then present their own version that carries an emotional and persuasive quality.

This persuasive strategy falls between fact and fiction into the realm of dramatic narratives. It explains events by giving them a shared meaning that makes a connection with the public to create and maintain their version of social reality.

Much of how social reality is constructed happens through dramatic narratives.

Chapter 2
Creating Social Reality to Win

Over time, many dramatic narratives can form a recognizable and meaningful view of society that creates social reality. It is the shared meaning that is found in dramatic narratives that can create social reality for people.

The power of social reality lies in its ability to explain our experiences and the world around us. It can be used to explain the motivation for people's behavior.

The sharing of social reality is a way of creating a common understanding of the world and how it works. Even though it may or may not accurately reflect actual reality, it may be no less real for them.

Social reality is created because people want to know about the world around them and social reality can be used to explain and predict physical reality.

Social reality can be as important to society as physical reality because much of human interaction and public institutions are socially constructed.

People want to know why the economy is bad and when it will get better. In an election, people want to know what they can expect from their government and what the government expects from them.

Social reality is attractive because it can explain seemingly chaotic events by telling people what is happening to them and how they fit into the grand scheme of things. It can also foster public confidence in a government by reducing uncertainty about it.

The use of social reality derives from the human need to reduce uncertainty by explaining events to make sense of them.

People often prefer a reality they have created themselves because they are more comfortable when it is made up of familiar elements of their own design.

Social reality tells people how to act and communicate with other people. It tells them what behaviors are accepted and which ones are not. It is a comprehensive explanation of how things work in society.

As people begin to exchange ideas they share dramatic narratives and a collective social reality begins to form that communicates who they are and what they are about.

When people are a part of a group, a more specialized version of social reality is developed to define the group and its members. This explains who are members and who are not, how one becomes a member, and establishes group values.

Social reality is attractive because is provides an easy and convenient way to explain and understand complex, chaotic circumstances. It reduces uncertainly and inspires confidence to give people a feeling of safety and stability.

There are many examples of specialized forms of social reality found in politics, religion, and culture. These specialized versions usually fit into the larger societal social reality.

Social reality can be restrictive as it can be a means of social control by influencing or motivating people's behavior, however, it also serves to provide stability without which society could not function.

A specialized version of social reality provides a way for those who share it to interpret actual reality to determine what it means for them. This meaning may be interpreted differently by different groups.

In the politics, there are many of these groups including conservatives, liberals, Democrats, Republicans, Independents, and moderates.

Groups seek not only to establish their own identity, but they also seek to convert new members to their movement who share their version of social reality.

Many political, religious, and social groups have sought to further their cause by moving larger groups of people to action through the creation of shared meaning.

Social reality is a powerful force because it tells people how to interpret physical reality and what to do about it.

Candidates develop their own specialized version of social reality to share meaning with the voters. This shared meaning can be developed by the candidate and their campaign team over time or it can be created spontaneously in the media and with the public.

Candidates share their own meanings when they communicate dramatic narratives about themselves, the opposition, the voters, and the campaign. This creates a group culture that can determine their electoral success or failure.

Candidates might create a culture that is open to new information and ideas, including listening to the people. However, all to often they become closed off, becoming arrogant having an attitude that they know what they are doing.

People who have different ideas or try to help them might be castigated as a nuisance and ignored or even met with hostility. This type of culture is likely to end in defeat because it reduces their ability to share meaning with the voters.

Conversion of Social Reality

In order to gain support, politicians must get people to share their version of social reality. Some people are predisposed to them, however, others share a different version of social reality.

When people have a different social reality, they must first be separated from their attachment to the version they currently share.

To accomplish this, their current version of social reality is attacked as repugnant or outdated. They are shown how wrong and misguided they really are.

Their previously shared dramatic narratives are called racist, sexist, xenophobic, homophobic, misogynist, or bigoted. They may be characterized as serial liars or haters. They may even be compared to communists or Nazis.

This approach is used to get people to reject their current version of social reality, because no one wants to be associated with these negative qualities. They are told their values are repugnant, so they need to change them.

When a person's social reality is attacked, they may begin to question it. They may feel lost or angry. They may begin looking for a new version of social reality.

Once they are persuaded that their old beliefs are wrong, they may feel the need to find a new version of social reality. So, they experience a period of internal conflict. This is when a new version of social reality is presented to them.

The new version is often characterized in positive qualities like being fair, just, doing what's right, or open minded. It may be characterized as right, considerate, enlightened, environmental, politically correct, egalitarian, or superior.

After a while, the new social reality may fall into place and they see things in a new way. When the conversion process ends, they may feel relieved their conflict is resolved.

They may show their commitment to the new social reality with some kind of action like volunteering, giving money, or voting. This is how people are motivated to do what others want them to do.

After a version of social reality has emerged and attracted followers, there is the problem of maintaining their commitment. Some groups are able to keep their social reality stable over long periods of time, while others suffer from decline and decay, or it may come to an end.

The process of keeping a version of social reality together is accomplished through ongoing shared meaning of dramatic narratives.

This serves to keep the people who share the vision committed by maintaining their adherence to it as well as to bring back those who have fallen away.

People who have fallen away might be criticized and pressured to conform to the new social reality. This is done by comparing an individual's undesirable behavior and bad character to the ideals contained in the new social reality.

The objective is to encourage recognition of their shortcomings, followed by repentance and a renewed commitment to the new social reality. This process can help to bring those who lose the vision back in line to conform to the demands of the new version of social reality.

How widely a candidate's social reality is shared can be reflected in their own dramatic narratives. One method of observing how well they are shared is though repetition of a particular story. During the course of a campaign, candidates try to reflect on how their messages are being received by the voters.

When one catches on with the public, it tends to be repeated and when they do not catch on with the public, they are more likely to be dropped.

No single speech or television ad is likely to sway the outcome of a campaign. It is the consistent weaving together of many forms of political discourse utilizing familiar dramatic narratives that share meaning with the voters that determines electoral success.

Social reality can be powerful because it tells people how to interpret physical reality and what to do about it. It can be used to explain events by telling people what is happening to them and how they fit in. It tells them what behaviors are accepted and which ones are not.

Social reality has a larger, more important function, it can affect who we are as an individual and what kind of person we want to be. It can determine who we are as a people and what kind of nation we want to be. It can inspire people to fight for a cause and for what they feel is right.

At one time our government and social institutions were an idea shared by people, sometime in the past. It is their vision of what society should be that shaped the world we live in today.

It is the shared meanings we have today that will determine what kind of world future generations will live in tomorrow.

Chapter 3
Creating Dramatic Narratives to Win

Election after election demonstrates the importance of a candidate creating their version of social reality and skillfully communicating it to the voters to legitimize their right to govern.

This process can be more important to a candidate's political fortunes than their positions on issues, popularity, credibility, or even past experience.

For instance, an incumbent with the most experience and the highest initial popularity of all the candidates, who lacks of a coherent or articulate version of social reality that shares meaning with the voters will sharply reduce their legitimacy to win.

A newcomer inexperienced in national politics or foreign affairs, may overcome obstacles by crafting compelling dramatic narratives as part of a panoramic version of social reality and then repeating them until they become widely shared with the public.

Initially, a newcomer has virtually no issue positions, yet if they craft a coherent version of social reality they are more likely to improve in the polls.

This demonstrates the importance of utilizing a clear version of social reality made up of artistically crafted dramatic narratives that will share meaning with the voters.

A candidate must characterize themselves and events in their version of social reality to legitimize their right to govern. They also must try to undermine their opponent's legitimacy by increasing uncertainty about them in the minds of the voters.

This can be accomplished through negative dramatic narratives about their opponent to try to separate the voters from their existing version of social reality, so that they will no longer support the other candidate.

This can leave a void that voters look to have filled, opening the way for a candidate to replace the old version with their new version of social reality.

A newcomer can more easily vilify the government as corrupt and repugnant to motivate people who have held the incumbent's version of social reality to reject it.

Then, they can then replace it with their version. An incumbent will lose vital support if they do not defend or support their version of social reality when this occurs.

A candidate must seek legitimacy by creating a connection with commonly recognized and established sources of credibility for their candidacy through party endorsements, political conventions, running in primaries, and by having won previous elections.

The sharing of communal values can be accomplished through populist mandates to demonstrate the people's support. This is most commonly accomplished by citing past elections and being re-elected to office as proof that a candidate represents the people and has their support.

Social reality is a powerful legitimizing force because it helps candidates explain who they are, what they stand for, and why they are running for office.

Candidates characterize themselves as personifying deeply held and well-established values and beliefs they hold in common with the people they want to represent.

Using dramatic narratives can help them to share meaning with the voters by connecting their political principles to the traditional values of the past and to unify the audience behind those values. This serves to reduce uncertainty about themselves, so that voters can feel comfortable voting for them.

Conversely, candidates might attack an opponent by showing how the political principles of their opponent are alien or repugnant to the traditional values of the people. They do this to create uncertainty about their opponent in the minds of the voters to help to defeat them.

Voters are more likely to be motivated to vote against someone with a high degree of uncertainty than for someone with a low degree of uncertainty because uncertainty can make people uncomfortable.

When people are uncomfortable they are more likely to do something about it, like voting. The more intense the feelings, the more motivated they can become.

If you want to motivate people to do something, make them angry or fearful. This is why negative campaigning is effective.

Shared Meaning Through Dramatic Narratives

In order to legitimize their right to govern, a candidate must create their version of social reality. Then, they must make a connection with the voters, usually through the media, and communicate their message to them so that they will understand it.

This is commonly done through the use of dramatic narratives, which are a persuasive telling of events often based on a few facts or events that are characterized in a manner that is neither factual nor fictional, but somewhere in between.

During a campaign, candidates create many dramatic narratives. When the public hears or sees these dramatic narratives, a connection is made and the candidate and the voter share meaning because they both understand what these dramatic narratives mean.

The process of shared meaning is essential to a campaign because it is how a candidate motivates voters not only to vote, but also to support them by campaigning, donating money, or volunteering for them.

By sharing meaning, ideas that exist in a person's (or candidate's) mind can motivate behavior creating actual physical reality. Sharing meaning is a powerful process because it has the potential to change perceptions and expectations, as well as motivate behavior.

It could be said that rhetorical forms fall into two categories, fact and fiction. There is the inherent assumption that if a candidate is not telling the truth they are lying.

If fact comprises those things that are verifiably true, and fiction is an imaginative creation developed through invention that does not represent actual reality, candidates who share meaning through dramatic narratives utilize neither fact nor fiction.

Instead, they take an inherent reality, like the economy or health care, select a few pertinent items and present a dramatic narrative that is their characterization interpreted to fit into their version of social reality. This maneuvering between fact and fiction falls within the realm of dramatic narratives.

Dramatic narratives explain events to create and maintain shared meaning with the public and to support a candidate's version of social reality.

Much of political social reality is constructed through dramatic narratives because they are more interesting and compelling for the public. They include characterizations about the candidate, their opponent, and the circumstances in the country.

For example, both Gulf Wars were initially considered a success. However, over time politicians have recast them in a more negative light, until they became perceived as foreign policy failures.

The events themselves did not change, only people's perception of them changed. Being able to exploit and adapt existing social reality and commonly shared meanings is essential to legitimating a candidate's right to govern.

Candidates often exploit established dramatic narratives that have been well defined in society like restoration, rebirth, and the American Dream. This helps to make their version of social reality easily understood since the electorate already knows them.

Over the course of a campaign, there are several dramatic narratives employed by candidates that are similar in nature. These narratives are often repeated throughout a campaign demonstrating that they shared meaning with the voters regardless of which candidate they supported. They are popular because people are already familiar with them making them easier to understand

The following section describes several well established dramatic narratives that candidates can utilize.

The American Dream Dramatic Narrative

The American Dream is an old and powerful dramatic narrative that characterizes America as the land of opportunity where anyone can realize his or her potential.

It originates from the Declaration of Independence that proclaims "all men are created equal" and have the right to the "pursuit of happiness." The American Dream is about everyone having the opportunity to be successful and prosper from their own work.

America is a place where everyone is equal regardless of who they are or where they came from. It is about an upwardly mobile society where the next generation will be better off than the last.

It is the hope of parents that their children will have it better than they did. It can also include benefits like getting a college education, having a good job, or home ownership.

The American Dream dramatic narrative is used by candidates because it is familiar to practically everyone, including people all over the world. It is so powerful that it motivated millions of people to leave their homes and seek a better life in America.

Candidates will often claim that they are running for office to restore the American Dream for our children because they can no longer stand by and let the next generation become the first to be worse off than their parents.

This dramatic narrative is primarily action driven as it is the candidate's actions and achievements that are characterized as enabling the realization of the American Dream.

In order to fulfill the promise of the American Dream, a candidate may call for a new type of leadership to reinvent government, so it can meet the challenges the people face. They may say that the American Dream has been destroyed by their opponent or the government that has lost touch with the people and their values.

A candidate includes the people in their dramatic narrative by saying that the people need the courage to reject the failed policies of the past and embrace their vision of the future, so together they can restore the American Dream.

A candidate may characterize themselves as the personification of the American Dream. They understand the people since they are one of them. This makes them qualified to help the people achieve and keep their own version of the American Dream.

During the campaign, a candidate may say that they always will remember the small town where they came from. Connecting this dramatic narrative of their hometown to the nation, a candidate might say that they still believe in the promise of America.

It is this dramatic narrative of typical small town Americana that can serve as the basis for their definition of the American Dream because it shares meaning with many people.

A newcomer or outsider can employ a similar version of the American Dream dramatic narrative. In their version, they may set themselves up as an example of someone who has the good fortune to live and benefit from the American Dream.

They may include examples of their personal realization of the American Dream in their dramatic narrative. Now they want to pass it on to our children and to their children. The focus of their version is on future generations and not as much on the present or past.

By including the dramatic narrative of the mess in government, a newcomer can support their contention that the American Dream is under siege. The growing national debt and the unwillingness of government to do anything about it has mortgaged our children's future to threaten the American Dream.

A candidate may employ the American Dream dramatic narrative when they tell stories about their early days, of how they began their business, got married, raised children, and came into public service.

This experience is often characterized as preparing them to help solve the problems of the country. However, now the American Dream as under attack by a villainous government that destroyed individual freedoms. Fundamental American values are being eroded by a government that is out of control and no longer represents the people.

The American Dream can be threatened by tax and spend liberals or extremist conservatives. So, the nation needs a candidate to protect the people from those who will destroy individual freedom and raised taxes.

The American Dream is based on empowering all people to make their own choices and to reach their potential by offering economic opportunity. The American Dream is a place where people can find a better life for themselves and their children. It is the American Dream that has made America the most dynamic society in the world.

Rebirth Dramatic Narrative

The rebirth dramatic narrative focuses on a person who experiences a defining moment that dramatically changes the direction of their life. The circumstances of the moment of rebirth are often told in detail and characterized in a dramatic style.

Candidates use this dramatic narrative to describe a pivotal moment in their own life that brought them into public service or to run for office.

Throughout the campaign, a candidate may characterize a defining moment in their life as when they realized their destiny was in public service. They may characterize this event as a symbolic passing of the torch that led them into public service and to run for office.

This conversion helps them to be sanctified by the people as their choice. They may utilize several different versions of the rebirth dramatic narrative in their campaign.

They might describe several experiences as a defining moment in their life. Meeting someone famous, a political figure, getting married, beginning a new life, raising a family, or starting a business that taught them valuable lessons they carried into public life.

This event motivated them to run in their first election launching a life of public service. Although these experiences are frequently described throughout the campaign, how they motivated them to pursue a life of public service and run for office must be clearly conveyed.

Candidate frequently utilize a number of dramatic narratives to legitimize their right to govern. They will use the rebirth dramatic narrative by characterizing the events that brought them into public service to explain why they are running for office.

This dramatic narrative can serve as a sanctifying agent to legitimize their seeking office. It helps to provide the basis of a populist mandate by presenting them as a candidate that understands the problems of ordinary people because they are one of them who has suffered similar problems.

The rebirth dramatic narrative has a long history in secular and religious rhetoric. It focuses on a person who experiences a defining moment in their life that changes it forever.

For the person who uses the rebirth dramatic narrative, it often begins with them living an aimless life. Then comes a dramatic experience that is characterized as a defining moment that changes the direction of their life.

The circumstances of the moment of their rebirth are often recounted in detail and are characterized in a dramatic narrative style.

In early America, evangelical ministers would recount their personal conversion experience of being born again or receiving the call to the ministry as an example of their faith to congregants and potential converts.

The rebirth dramatic narrative is important to a candidate because if it is shared with the public, it can help to legitimize their right to govern.

A candidate who uses the rebirth dramatic narrative will tell about how their life has changed, often giving details of when and how it occurred. It is characterized as a defining moment in their life that motivated them to begin a purposeful life of public service.

A photo of the defining moment can also be used as a symbolic image to help legitimize their claim to office.

A candidate will tell about their experience attending school and about what their faith means to them. They may characterize their campaign as one to restore hope by bringing people together because we are all in this together.

A candidate may include their version of the restoration dramatic narrative by urging the country to embrace a renewal of the American spirit to bring it together with a greater sense of community.

They may tell how grateful they are for being born in a country where people have religion in their lives, a country made great by religious freedom.

This freedom is a tribute to the genius and the courage of the American experiment because the government can be the protector of the freedom of every faith.

Restoration Dramatic Narrative

Restoration is an old and familiar dramatic narrative that is frequently utilized by candidates during an election campaign.

The attraction of the restoration dramatic narrative is in its ability to maintain previously shared meanings by keeping them intact, while simultaneously calling for change.

There are times when people feel that in order to move forward to a better future, they need to go back to the past in order to restore something good that has been lost.

The restoration dramatic narrative begins in the past when times are good and people are virtuous. Then there comes a time of troubles that brings on the problems that exist today.

They may feel that their problems are due to the people losing their way or that their leaders have become corrupted, so things can be resolved by returning to the values of the past.

The restoration dramatic narrative has both sacred and secular versions. As a part of their social reality, speakers in both the religious and political realms have utilized the restoration dramatic narrative.

The sacred version is based on Jesus and their disciples establishing the values and principles for the Christian Church. The subsequent failure of the church did not result in the rejection of Christianity, but is instead seen as a falling away from the values of the church.

The restoration dramatic narrative calls for a return to the original foundation of the church. Throughout history, when a society experienced a time of troubles, it is often interpreted as evidence of a divine message that it has lost its way and must return to its original values.

The secular version of restoration is based on the values and principles established by the original founders of the nation. The subsequent failure of the government and society to uphold those principles is seen not as a failure of the system of government, but rather a falling away from the true principles upon which the nation is founded.

Restoration requires changing our current ways and returning to traditional values and principles that have been forsaken.

This dramatic narrative serves as a secular depiction of the heritage of government based on the glorification of a golden age sometime in the past. All who participate in the dramatic narrative share a common social bond as well as a bond with the founders of the institution being restored.

In an election campaign, the restoration dramatic narrative often begins with a depiction of a time of troubles. So, in order to demonstrate a sense of purpose for their candidacy, a candidate must characterize the present as a time of troubles caused by years of neglect that created the need for restoration.

This troubled time provides the motive for change and the restoration dramatic narrative allows for a reform movement to develop that would correct the evils of society and reaffirm people's faith in the institutions of society without destroying them.

At various times in history, when people suffered a time of hardship they interpreted it as a falling away from their true values. Even today, when people face a time of troubles there arises a movement to change the corrupt present by returning to the ideals of the past.

By restoring the ideals and values of the past, people will resolve their problems to improve their present condition.

A variation of restoration is the founding. Many groups have a founding dramatic narrative that tells the story of how a group, organization, a people, or a nation came into existence. It includes dramatic narratives about how and why it was formed and the notable people in its history.

The founding is important because it is more than just a recounting of the past, it tells what a group of people stands for, what kind of people belong to it, and how they are expected to behave. For example, the American founding dramatic narrative tells how America began, the qualities of the people who founded it, and what it means to be an American.

When groups, organizations, or nations find themselves in difficult times, they might utilize restoration as a means of returning to the values and principles of their founding and their founders to restore what made it great. Restoration can be characterized as a means of 'societal rebooting.'

In an election campaign, candidates utilize restoration as a means of legitimizing their candidacy and undermining their opponent. A challenger may characterize the incumbent or the party in power as corrupt, having fallen away from the values of the people. If the newcomer is elected, they will restore the government to the values that made it great before the current incumbent was elected.

This is how a newcomer can drive a wedge between their opponent and the voters by asserting that their opponent has strayed, been corrupted, or is no longer consistent with the values of the people and so they must be replaced.

During a campaign, a candidate might utilize the founding dramatic narrative, which is a variation of restoration. Restoration relies on basic principles of freedom and equality set forth in the founding of America and personified by its current and past leaders.

A candidate must share the communal values that they personify by calling for restoration of the principles and values that America is founded upon and that made it great.

Change can be used as a variation of restoration because it is necessary to change the people in government in order to restore the original ideals set out by the founders.

Many candidates employ restoration in their version of social reality as an action based dramatic narrative centered around themselves as the hero or agent of change who will restore the government to the people based on the traditions and values established at the founding of our nation.

They may also characterize the present government as being corrupt and their opponent as having no vision, leadership, or strategy. This is a government that practiced divisiveness, so it is in need of reform.

The restoration dramatic narrative refers to restoring the bond between the people and the government. It is founded on the values and principles of the nation that have been lost. The country needs a leader with a new approach to restore these values, so we can resolve the problems facing the people.

A candidate must include the voters in their restoration narrative. They may characterize the election as a crusade to help people and to restore the middle class.

They will restore America to its former greatness by creating jobs and rewarding hardworking families that have been abandoned by their government.

They will also restore fairness to the tax system, legal system, and health care system. In revolutionizing government, they are the agent of change who will restore the government to the people.

Throughout the campaign, a candidate may call for change to restore America. Change can mean a change in themselves from old style politicians, a change that rejects the failed policies of the past, and a change in government to help the people.

In order to restore the nation, people must have the courage to change. It is through change that restoration can be realized, so the people can have a better future.

It is through change that the principles and values of the past can be restored to the government, to the people, and to the nation.

In a newcomer's case, restoration is a call back to the people's values drawing upon their traditions because the government is full of corruption and disarray because our elected representatives have forgotten the people who sent them there.

Utilizing several references to the falling away from traditional values, a candidate might imply much about the current state of the country and the failure of the other candidates to help the people.

Thus, they create a reason to restore the government by acknowledging the public's growing disillusion with the other candidates to legitimize their own candidacy.

In establishing their legitimacy, a candidate might develop many dramatic narratives that utilize restoration to convince voters to support them. It is the people's role to restore the government to correct the evil without impairing what is good.

A candidate can justify their running for office based on the restoration of basic values in government by addressing the issues that are important to the people.

A candidate and the people represent the means by which this restoration can take place. They can connect with the voters by using restoration to evoke communal values that epitomized the people's principles, linking their values with their own.

An incumbent may allude to restoration by telling of returning to the work they started some time ago. This dramatic narrative suggests that somehow they have been driven off course and now must return to an earlier mission.

A candidate must create a strong vision of what America will look like after it has been restored under their leadership. They may compare the restoration of freedom and democracy abroad to the need to restore individual freedom from government at home.

A candidate must cast themselves as the central hero in their dramatic narratives who will restore the government to the people by fighting the villains out to destroy all the people value.

With the people's help they will restore the government to basic values that will empower the people. A candidate also alludes to restoration when they say that government is too big and costs too much.

Vision of a Better Future Dramatic Narrative

In order to legitimize their right to govern, a candidate has to create their vision of the future. This vision serves to represent the their purpose for seeking office and what they hope to accomplish if they win.

If a candidate cannot clearly articulate their vision of the future, the people will question why they are running for office.

Having a vision of the future is important because it serves to reduce uncertainty about a candidate. Candidates can accomplish this in one of two ways.

First, they may characterize their past successes and accomplishments. They may claim that they can replicate their past successes. They develop their vision of the future based on their political or legislative accomplishments.

The second way is to make the future appear better by downgrading the present. They may characterize present conditions as intolerable with the people suffering and the country falling apart.

The purpose is to degrade the present to make the vision of the future as attractive as possible. This is perhaps why candidates recast the past as a time of greed and irresponsibility, whether it has any basis in fact or not.

Once the people are aware of how bad things really are, they will welcome a change. This process can be analogous to the evangelical process of a religious conversion.

When a person's current version of social reality is characterized as repugnant or wrong, it can motivate them to question and eventually abandon it. This can leave a void that creates an opportunity to present a new social reality to replace their old one. This is how candidates can persuade people to support and vote for them.

The Persecuted Victim Dramatic Narrative

The persecuted victim is an old and familiar dramatic narrative in American rhetoric. Many individuals and groups have characterized their problems as the consequence of being unjustly victimized by the system or persecuted by villains out to destroy them.

During the course of a campaign, a candidate may be hit with scandals over their personal conduct. In this case they may employ this narrative to cast their accusers as villains who are out to not only hurt them, but to hurt the people as well.

For the most part, judging by public opinion, these narratives work.

In this situation, a candidate must characterize their attackers as villains who are dishonest, unjustly persecuting others for their own personal gain. These villains cannot win an honest debate, so they must resort to underhanded tactics abhorrent to the people's values.

It is the people who will suffer because they have to answer these accusations rather than addressing more important issues.

When a candidate is hit with accusations, they must try to defuse the sharing of these dramatic narratives because they can have a powerful attraction for the media and the public.

If they are widely shared, they could well end their candidacy, so more direct measures are often needed to save their campaign. In past elections, candidates had their careers cut short over this by failing to properly respond.

A candidate can fight back by characterizing themselves as being unjustly persecuted, their accusers as being dishonest, pursuing their own agenda of distracting the people from the important issues facing the country, and derailing their candidacy.

In response to accusations, a candidate might appear on television refute the allegations. Their strategy might be to not respond directly to the accusations leveled against them.

They are not likely to answer the accusations directly, but rather spin out a series of dramatic narratives in which they appeal to the public to respect and preserve their family's private life.

A candidate may respond by characterizing their accusers and the press as exploiting them and their family for their own gain. In turn, they attack the press and blame them for trying to get them.

In responding to scandals and accusations, a candidate must shift the focus from a question of credibility to reaffirming their version of social reality by characterizing these accusations as not only personal attacks on them, but on the American people as well.

They are in the race for the people, not to debate their private personal issues. A self-serving group of villains are sensationalizing events for their own personal gain at the people's expense.

Defending themselves from these accusations has distracted their time and energy from addressing more important issues. The people want their problems solved and are not interested in their personal life, because it has little bearing on their ability to get things done. Past dramatic narratives can be quickly employed and stressed to divert attention from the scandal.

It is likely that the public will respond by feeling that the candidate is being unfairly treated by the media and that the matter has nothing to do with their ability to do the job. This can help to defuse a potentially dangerous sharing of negative dramatic narratives about them.

When a negative dramatic narrative is characterized in the media, it is more likely to be shared by the public.

In order to control the damage, a candidate needs to respond by developing their version of the persecuted victim dramatic narrative to become a part of their version of social reality.

This dramatic narrative reaffirmed past dramatic narratives of American values that are upheld and shared with the people. Whenever their version of social reality subsequently came under attack, the persecuted victim dramatic narrative can be used to support their version of social reality.

In each case, a candidate may characterize themselves as an unjustly persecuted victim by using dramatic narratives, only changing the characters and plot lines to meet each situation.

They may characterize each dramatic narrative as a conflict between good and evil, and the unfair tactics of villains out for personal gain who victimized them.

Meanwhile, a candidate thought only about the good of the people. Attacks on them are instigated by those who are trying to stop their program to help people, so these attacks are victimizing the people themselves.

This approach casts the candidate as the hero in these dramatic narratives because they stand between these villains and the people heroically fighting for them, which can represent the unjust persecution of the people by these villains.

This image serves to reinforce their version of social reality and attract public support as the people come to realize that their campaign must be defended.

When a candidate's dramatic narratives are primarily action based and not persona based, accusations surrounding their character are secondary to what they want to do to help the people.

This may account for why a candidate might have negative personal ratings and yet gain public support against their opponents.

Chapter 4
Changing Social Reality to Win

Any version of social reality must be maintained or it will decay naturally on its own over time. When a version of social reality comes under attack by people who seek to pry the supporters who share to from it, so they can convert them to their own version, it must be defended.

If an incumbent fails to defend their version of social reality when it comes under attack, they will have difficultly maintaining the people's support.

If a version of social reality is not maintained or defended when attacked, the supporters who share it will begin to question why they should continue to believe in it. They will question why they should have this view of social reality when their leaders don't support them.

Society and social reality

The power of social reality can be a significant motivating force that influences the development of society. It does this by creating expectations of what is considered acceptable behavior, enforced with rewards and punishments.

Social reality can be a positive force encouraging people to develop new ideas, inspire creativity, encourage innovation, motivate people to take action, and communicate ideas with one another.

When a society becomes removed from the social reality that made it great, it can begin to fragment leading to competing factions that can cause it to deteriorate.

When increasing numbers of people become more discon-nected, they are less able to communicate or share meaning.

When segments of society try to impose their specialized ver-sion of social reality on others, it can lead to societal fragmentation, which can undermine society so it declines and decays.

Social reality has changed in the past, so it will change in the future. When the existing social reality changes, what will take its place?

Changing Social Reality

Throughout history people have changed their social reality in-cluding the structures and institutions of society. Even today, we see different cultures and countries taking very different approaches to how they structure society.

There can be some people and groups who try to change social reality to achieve their own goals by motivating others to do what they want them to do.

In order to change social reality, they will first try to detach oth-ers from their current social reality. This can be done by character-izing the old social reality as outdated, backward, or out of touch.

If they can be detached from their old social reality, there will be a void created that they will feel motivated to fill.

When people are looking for answers they can be more open to a new version social reality. This is when a candidate might try to convince them that their way is the right way by providing them a new version of social reality.

The following are some methods that have been used to change social reality in groups, organizations, and society to achieve spe-cific desired outcomes.

Some methods can be helpful, while others can be considered manipulative. It is helpful to have an awareness of how they work because of how they can be utilized.

Communicate the need for change

How much people are willing to change depends upon their needs and wants, perceptions and expectations, and the amount of uncertainty they will tolerate before they are motivated to resolve it. They are unlikely to change something that is familiar unless they perceive doing so will improve their situation or relieve tension.

People can be more likely to change if the need for change is communicated along with the reasons why the current situation is undesirable, and failure to change it will result in serious consequences.

Get people involved

Giving people something to do helps them to feel that they have an investment in the process, which can make them more likely to support it. One of the main reasons that programs and policies fail or don't get support is that the public is not given a role with something to do.

If the outcome is linked to their self-concept, then they have a stake in its success and are more likely to work for a successful outcome. It's easy to criticize what others do, but it's more difficult to criticize something when you are a part of it.

Set achievable goals

People have an easier time making small incremental changes rather than large ones. The degree of change that is acceptable to someone is based upon their perception of the current situation before the change and their perception of the situation afterwards. If the difference is small, it is less perceptible making it more acceptable.

Things have to change and most change takes place within reasonable limits. If the change is too big, it is more likely to be opposed because it increases uncertainty above what is acceptable.

Communicate a positive vision

Engage people's imagination by creating a view of the future that is better than today. This can motivate people to change by portraying it as helping to fulfill their needs and wants by providing them with benefits.

A positive vision of the future can be compared to a negative vision where everyone will be worse off if there is no change. This can help to reduce feelings of apprehension about what change will be like in the future.

Present an opportunity

The notion of opportunity can be a powerful motivator for change because people want to improve their situation. Seizing this opportunity can help them demonstrate their intelligence, courage, or open mindedness. It can be used as a way to provide them with benefits.

Make connections

People are more likely to communicate with those who are in close proximity, who share similar backgrounds, are involved in doing similar tasks, or with whom they come in frequent contact.

To get people to communicate with one another, find a way to make a connection between them. This can be being in close proximity, having a mutual interest, or finding a common activity. This can help them make connections to provide support.

Utilize social pressure

Encourage change by creating social pressure because people want to get along with others and fit in. When a person's behavior fits in with the norms of a group or society, others are more comfortable investing their resources in them because it reduces uncertainty.

People can be motivated to change by appealing to their need for acceptance and inclusion. They are more likely to change and engage in behaviors that are considered socially acceptable because they perceive that by conforming they will have needs and wants fulfilled.

Utilize resources

Change can be encouraged by motivating people and organizations that provide resources to support for those who encourage change. Resources like money, can provide a strong motivation for change.

If a group or individual resists change, they may be persuaded by identifying their needs and wants, and either fulfilling them or cutting them off from others who fulfill them.

Appeal to fairness

People like to be perceived as being reasonable and open minded rather than disagreeable or closed minded. This approach can be used to motivate people to get them to do what others want them to do, sometimes for their own gain.

When people are reluctant or resist doing what others want them to do, they may try to motivate them by characterizing them as closed minded, unfair, disagreeable, obstructionist, discriminatory, haters, or troublemakers, whether they are or not.

Create a diversion

Magicians use sleight of hand to divert attention to perform their illusions. In the movies, when a character wants to do something that they don't want others to notice, they create a diversion to distract attention from their actions.

People filter out information they do not find useful. They make choices about what information to perceive. To help implement change, create a message that gets people's attention, so they will be encouraged to change.

Uncertainty can give the perception that there is a need for change by making people uncomfortable. If people think there is increasing instability due to uncertainty, they are likely to become increasingly uncomfortable motivating them to take action. They may even want government or some other authority to restore stability.

People can be motivated to change if they are faced with a potential threat that could undermine their safety and security.

Present a plan

If there is the perception that the current situation is unsustainable, it can increase uncertainty motivating people to want to take action to reduce it. They are likely to support a plan that reduces uncertainty if it makes things easier for them.

If there is opposition, a candidate might say that the time for talk is over, it's time to take action. This is done so people do not have time to form their own ideas.

Use negativity

Characterizing something as negative can be more motivating than being positive. This is because if circumstances are perceived as being positive, uncertainty will likely be reduced so there is little discomfort to motivate people to change.

Negativity can make people feel more uncomfortable increasing uncertainty making circumstances less tolerable motivating them to do something about it, so that they will feel more comfortable. One way people motivate others to change is to make them angry or uncomfortable by increasing uncertainty to the point where it's no longer tolerable.

This can be done by portraying circumstances as increasingly uncertain and unstable, so the desired change must be implemented. People are more likely to change things they perceive as intolerable, unacceptable, or harmful, whether they are or not.

Use emotion

Emotion can be a powerful motivating force for change. People are more likely to be moved by emotion than logic because it appeals to personal needs and wants.

We all want to feel good, that we can make a difference, and that we are a good person who does the right thing.

Emotion is often used when rational appeals do not work or are not as effective. Common emotional appeals include sympathy, empathy, anger, and fear.

Using some of these methods can be risky because they could make people feel that they are being manipulated.

The ticking bomb

Movies create drama and tension by showing a ticking bomb while the hero tries to find it and disarm it. In social reality, some people may use a false crisis or an impending artificial deadline to create tension or drama to provide motivation for change.

Change is presented as the only way to diffuse the perceptual 'ticking bomb.' If the prescribed change is not implemented as rapidly as possible or before the false deadline, dire consequences will result.

For instance, programs are more likely to be supported if the fate of the world is at stake rather than if it's a good thing to do. This approach is meant to create an emotional visceral reaction, rather than a rational analysis of the situation.

Repetition makes right.

To get people's attention, politicians have to repeat their messages many times. Being consistent gives the impression of confidence, but constantly changing a message gives the impression they are unsure of themselves. However, repeating misinformation can create the impression that it is true.

Use the past

The past can be more familiar making it attractive increasing uncertainty about future change. So, people may try to alter perceptions casting the old way in negatives terms or as unsustainable. They will try to reduce the perception of uncertainty about the new way.

They may characterize change using attractive qualities such as being innovative, environmental, open minded, progressive, or cost effective whether it is or not. This can increase uncertainty about the old way and anyone who supports it.

Use traditions and rituals

Traditions and rituals are a way that we share meaning to keep the past relevant today and for the future. Shared meaning tells us what is important in society, it helps share mutual expectations, and it creates common ground.

Traditions and rituals help people to share meaning to communicate what is important and valued by society. It is the means by which we invest words, symbols, and behaviors with meaning. While most of these things develop naturally over time, they can also be artificially created or altered to facilitate change.

Traditions and rituals help to reduce uncertainty by sharing meaning about what it means to be a member of society. They help us to make connections with one another by sharing common values, experiences, and emotions to invest them with meaning.

Use listening

Listen to the people so that they feel like they have a say in the decisions that affect them. When others feel that they have a stake in the outcome, they can have a greater investment in creating and maintaining change.

If people have a stake in the outcome, they are more likely to support change. When they have a stake in the outcome, it increases the likelihood they will accept change.

Use needs and wants

People are motivated to take action to fulfill needs and wants, so they are more likely to respond to change if they feel that it fulfills them better than the ways of the past.

Change can be made permanent by fulfilling these needs and wants. If people feel that they are receiving fair rewards that meet their expectations, then they will focus less on the negative aspects of change.

The perception of future rewards can encourage them to implement change without expecting immediate rewards.

This can help people let go of the way they did things in the past by replacing them with something they perceive as beneficial in the future, so they can be more receptive to change.

Changing social reality

These are some examples of how some people and groups facilitate change. Changing social reality can benefit everyone if people are aware of what is happening and have a say in what it will become.

Rather than approaching change as negative, it can be a positive force for good to help people and improve their quality of life.

Chapter 5
Creating Legitimization to Win

An election campaign can be seen as a series of attempts to legitimize a candidate's right to govern and to undermine their opponent's legitimacy, in order to be elected to office.

During a campaign, there are some ways candidates use to legitimize their right to govern by using several sanctifying agents.

Political success often comes from how these sanctifying agents are used by a candidate to convince the people to vote for them.

This depends on what events are selected, how they are characterized, and what dramatic narratives are shared with the public.

The following section describes sanctifying agents that can be used by candidates to legitimize their right to govern.

The People

Candidates legitimize their right to govern by referring to following the will of the people. There can be an aversion to people who seek office for their own designs.

So, a candidate must seek office because they are following the will of the people or for the good of the people, often through self-sacrifice, but not to further their own goals or ambitions.

Candidates call upon the people by referring to their past service in office, winning past elections, being supported by ordinary people, grassroots organizations, and other populist mandates.

Candidates must find and communicate a compelling reason to draw support from the people or they will not win.

The people are always the hero in a candidate's dramatic narratives. The people are not criticized, no matter what the state of the nation or economy.

The nation's problems are never the fault of the people, even though they elected the folks who made the mess in government in the first place.

The candidates find the people not only an important sanctifying agent to legitimize their campaign, but also an agent of action in their dramatic narratives as it is the will of the people that will prevail.

The candidates often say that the people have the choice to elect the kind of government they want, yet the government they elect needs to be changed every election.

Candidates can use ordinary people as a form of proxy to attack their opponents in ways that they cannot do without running the risk of damaging their public persona.

Candidates need to be seen interacting with the people, from individuals to large crowds. Candidates often use television commercials showing them at campaign rallies surrounded by enthusiastic crowds.

Being seen around people shows that a candidate has wide spread support. When a candidate has meeting with a small turnout, it can be interpreted as their having little public support.

Candidates can use the testimonies of individuals to show that the people support them. Showing a candidate with the people, especially on social media, in television ads, and in news reports serves to legitimize them with the voters as a sanctifying agent.

Meeting with ordinary people shows that they are open and approachable, even if they really are not. Showing a candidate in front of large groups of people demonstrates that the people actively support a candidate and provides a critical visual element to share meaning with the voters. It is a means to show strength and political power.

This is why old-fashioned events like political rallies and shaking people's hands are still an important mainstay of election campaigns, even in a mass media age.

It is not enough to be chosen by the people, a candidate also has to be seen as being one of them. During a campaign, candidates go to great lengths to show how average they are. As a candidate creates a public persona the voters can empathize with, they come to emulate them in various ways.

Candidates must demonstrate they have the average person's tastes, so they participate in ordinary activities, that represents the average person's values and beliefs.

If the people are convinced a candidate is like them, they will be more likely to empathize with them and support the candidate because people tend to like candidates who they perceive are similar to themselves. If the people do not feel a candidate is like themselves, they can be perceived as out of touch or elitist.

A candidate's version of social reality must be relatively stable to reduce uncertainty, while being flexible enough to account for change. Having shared meaning based on the people allows for new dramatic narratives and a version of social reality that can adapt to changing circumstances.

To help legitimize their candidacy, a candidate will call upon the people. In claiming a populist mandate, they will establish a government that will come directly from the people and be in their best interest.

In characterizing their purpose for running for office, candidates employ several dramatic narratives. The people are good, decent, and hardworking, but have been abandoned by the government, a government that has helped villains who did not share the values of most people.

Government should serve the people, rather than the people serve government.

In this respect, a candidate may say that they would make the people the focus of government because they know the people's troubles. They are close to the people and know their problems first hand because they share their hopes and dreams.

Candidates use these narratives to share meaning with people who feel that they have been abandoned by government, so they will return fairness to government by rewarding people who work hard and play by the rules.

If a candidate's version of social reality is primarily action oriented, whenever confronted by a crisis stemming from criticisms or scandal during the campaign, they can use the people as a means of damage control to deflect criticism. Many of their dramatic narratives share meaning around a candidate taking action on the people's behalf.

When unforeseen events like scandals and revelations about their past present themselves, a candidate can return to familiar dramatic narratives that have shared meaning with the public in order to defend themselves against these attacks and galvanize support.

A candidate can utilize commonly shared meanings by characterizing these attacks as attacks on the people themselves. They may depict this as preventing them from solving the people's problems.

This approach may help to attract supporters to defend themselves because they do not center on them, but rather on the people.

Throughout a campaign, an incumbent must claim a populist mandate based on the support of the people. Having run for office, an incumbent may have significant electoral success to demonstrate that they have the support of the people. This can be enhanced by showing them with people and in front of campaign rallies.

Even an incumbent needs to claim that the people have legitimized their right to govern. This can be shown by their level of support and approval in the polls.

However, an acknowledgment that the people want change or trying to characterize themselves as the agent of change can undermine them.

Candidates typically utilize popular mandates by reminding the people of their past elections and service in public office, to legitimize their right to govern. A newcomer cannot claim such a mandate, so they have to develop another sanctioning agent to fulfill this need.

As a result, a newcomer may take a different approach by creating the shared meaning of the accidental or reluctant candidate chosen by the people to run. In doing so, a newcomer creates a public persona of the candidate of the people who is drafted in a grassroots movement.

Initially, a newcomer might say that they will run only if the people want them to run. They may characterize their campaign not as a campaign, but as a grassroots movement because it furthers their populist image.

A newcomer may call on the people claiming that the other candidates are not addressing the issues that are important to the people, but instead are trivializing the election.

Saying that the people have spoken, a newcomer can enter the race to bolster their legitimacy. The heroes in their dramatic narratives are often the hardworking people who are now forgotten.

They often characterize the middle class as being under attack by government, so the next generation will not have the same quality of life as the last. Perhaps they refer to the middle class because it comprises the largest segment of voters.

A candidate may claim that ordinary people have asked them to run, so they can characterize themselves as a candidate of the people who owed nothing to anyone but them.

Characterizing themselves as the people's servant, a newcomer will give it everything they have to win. This approach places the people at the center of this dramatic narrative as the sanctifying agent.

Finally, a newcomer will call for the people's support. They can only run if the people are with them. They are doing this because they love their country, the people, and the principles on which it is founded. They didn't like to see those principles violated.

A newcomer must be the central character in their own action based dramatic narratives that can only be completed with the support of the people. It is up to them, the result is in their hands because the people own this country.

External Forces

In legitimizing their right to govern, candidates often call on forces outside themselves. These are meant to show the voters that the candidate has wide spread support. This can be very effective because people are often swayed by the opinions of others in choosing a candidate.

People have predispositions based on their version of social reality that can be as important or in some circumstances even more important than the actual candidates themselves.

People often vote for labels like party affiliations, ideology, or policies that can make the personal attributes of a candidate virtually inconsequential. This is evidenced by the fact that the voters support and elect candidates despite ongoing issues of character and experience that plague their campaign.

Throughout a campaign, a candidate can utilize dramatic narratives that share meaning with the voters. Some dramatic narratives contain sacred and religious overtones that call on spiritual forces outside of a candidate themselves.

A candidate must create a bond between themselves and the people founded on the values and principles of the nation. This forges their commitment to the people and creates their vision of government.

A candidate is the main agent who will return the government to the people by restoring the bond between themselves and the people. In order to restore the bond, there needs to be a change in how government conducts business, as well as a change of direction.

Change fits in with the dramatic narrative of restoration because it allows the government to be restored without altering its structure. Employing the restoration dramatic narrative recalls past traditions and values upon which America is founded, and change represents having faith in a better future.

A candidate often relies on their party's endorsement as a sanctifying agent. An incumbent will utilize the support of influential people like government and business leaders to support their candidacy.

Much has been made of the political advantages an incumbent candidate has over their challengers. Having been in office for years should legitimize their candidacy, but it should not be taken for granted.

A newcomer does not have traditional bases of support like party conventions, past elections, or incumbency. Instead, they must use the grassroots support of the people as their sanctifying agent. A newcomer must use other external sanctifying forces like the traditional values they share with the people and supporting the American Dream.

Candidates need to utilize external forces like endorsements from influential people, business and government leaders, celebrities, experts, and ordinary citizens. They may also use real and hypothetical characters cast as heroes and villains.

They may portray themselves as a hero fighting for the people against shadowy villains who are hurting the people, ruining the country, or destroying the American dream.

These villains can be their opponent, lobbyists, special interests, Washington insiders, Wall Street, big banks, as well as others.

Inner Forces

In legitimizing their right to govern, candidates often call on forces from within themselves. These can include the inner qualities of character, trustworthiness, experience, and the ability to get things done. They do this to show the voters that they are the best candidate for office.

The qualities voters consider important can vary based on how they are characterized in dramatic narratives. For instance, people may think honesty and trust matters for one candidate, but not for another. This is evidenced by voters not trusting some candidates, while feeling they have the best plan.

An incumbent's version of social reality serves to legitimize their right to govern by characterizing them as an experienced leader who has a plan to improve the government.

They may characterize themselves as a competent, effective leader, with government and business leaders endorsing their candidacy.

A candidate can utilize the rebirth dramatic narrative by telling stories of how they came to a life of public service. This experience can be characterized throughout the campaign as the defining moment that shaped their life.

A newcomer may imply that they can do for the people what they have done in government or business. They can be depicted as a hardworking and thoughtful leader who is genuinely interested in people and can get things done.

Their characterization of change should be presented as safe and not threatening to reduce uncertainty about them.

At first an incumbent will seek to legitimize their right to govern by characterizing themselves as an experienced leader. They will reiterate their accomplishments in the past to demonstrate that they can meet the challenges of the future.

When developing a right to govern, candidates often recall their record and experience to show that they can do the job in office. They will also call into question their opponent's judgment and character to increase uncertainty about their ability to govern and to make the difficult decisions they have to make.

In order to set themselves apart from their opponents, a newcomer may claim that they have no experience in creating the current problems. They are not a person who is wise in the ways of government, but they have learned to accomplish things in a way that the average person can identify with.

Politicians who have served in office use their record to gain legitimacy. If things have gone well, they will focus on their success as evidence they should be reelected.

If things have not gone well, they may claim the work they started has not been finished, so they need another term to get the job done.

An incumbent may say that now is not the time to elect someone untested or inexperienced, so we must stay the course. However, many incumbents have made the mistake of assuming that they would be re-elected simply because they are already in office thinking that the people will vote for them because they are familiar, rather than taking a chance on someone new.

Unexpected forces

While candidates and their campaign organizations plan how they create and communicate dramatic narratives to form their version of social reality, there are times when circumstances create them on their own.

There are also times when candidates connect with dramatic narratives that already exist in society. These can help as well as hinder their candidacy.

One element that can have an impact on a candidate's success is how they use music to inspire and motivate people. Music is a well established means of sharing meaning with the people to motivate behavior because it makes an emotional connection with them.

Many of the winning candidates have campaign theme songs that tied into the larger social reality. Music can serve as a form of dramatic narrative to share meaning with the voters to tell them what a campaign is about. It may also communicate a generational connection with the people.

Since the public has a wide variety of tastes in music, it is helpful to consider just what a song might communicate and who will share the meaning to help a candidate connect with their supporters.

Candidates share meaning with the voters through the colors and logos they chose to represent their campaign. The most common and effective are red, white, and blue. They often use graphic variations of the American flag as a logo because this appeals to the people's values and traditions, fulfilling their expectations.

Some candidates may use other colors to stand out from the crowd of candidates like yellow, green, or purple. However, colors and logos that diverge too much from those in the larger societal social reality are generally not as effective.

As much as political campaigns try to control events, they can be subject to unexpected forces. This can give them a high degree of uncertainty making them unpredictable. There can be a turn of events that creates shared meaning with the media and the public.

Problems do not take a holiday for an election. There can be events or a crisis that takes a candidate's attention away from the campaign. Some crisis comes from tragic events, protests, or natural disasters.

A candidate, especially an incumbent already in office, must take the time to address this crisis. They must go to the place where it occurs and been seen with the people who are affected.

While this may not actually accomplish anything not already being done, it shows they are actively engaged in solving the problem. It helps to instill confidence in people that they care and something is being done to help them.

Negative Campaigning

During every election there is the issue of negative campaigning and who slings the first handful of mud.

Just as literary forms like novels and movies use heroes and villains engaged in conflict to connect with an audience, political dramatic narratives utilize heroes to save the people from villains out to harm them.

Candidates utilize dramatic narratives to make voters fearful or angry of their opponent by characterizing them as a villain out to destroy the country and everything the people hold dear.

This can motivate people to withdraw their support of the opponent and vote against them. Voters are more likely to support a candidate who is cast as the hero, who will save them from a terrible fate or impending crisis.

Response to negative campaigning suggests that the voters encourage candidates to do it.

Negative campaigning serves to delegitimize an opponent by increasing the voters' perception of uncertainty about them. The more voters are uncertain about a candidate and what they will do, the more likely they are to be motivated to vote against them by voting for their opponent.

Negative campaigning can increase voter turnout. Low turnout may not necessarily be due to voter apathy, but the perception that either candidate will have the same result. They may not be uncomfortable enough with either candidate to be motivated to vote for any of them.

If an incumbent is a well-meaning person whose ideas aren't too bad just different, why vote to unseat them? If two candidates are well-meaning, but have different ideas, people can be less motivated to even vote at all.

The lack of voter turnout may be more due to the perception that electing either candidate will result in a similar outcome, rather than due to voter apathy.

Negative campaigning can be a powerful motivating force because people are more likely to vote against someone that makes them uncomfortable, angry, or fearful than to vote against someone who may be an okay candidate.

While this approach can be successful, it can increase divisions within society making governing more difficult.

The accusation of negative campaigning can be used to neutralize an opponent. If a candidate complains that their opponent is using unfair tactics or dirty tricks it can create a chilling effect motivating them to reduce or stop their negative ads, particularly if they are working and share meaning with the voters.

This can be an effective diversionary tactic to draw attention away from their own negative ads. A candidate can use this tactic effectively by accusing the incumbent of dirty tricks and being unfair, while running their own negative ads.

A candidate can interpret the intensity of their opponent's negative campaigning as a measure of how well their own dramatic narratives are being shared.

A candidate is more likely to attack and run negative ads against an opponent they perceive as a serious threat to their candidacy. A candidate will not likely expend resources against an opponent who poses little or not threat to their winning.

They will increase negative campaigning if their opponent is beating them or poses a threat to their winning. Complaining about a candidate's negative campaigning can be a form of negative campaigning in and of itself.

It is not negative campaigning to point out an opponent's shortcomings, failures, and weaknesses. This is part of the process of legitimizing a candidate and testing their fitness for office. However, there is an ethical line that should not be crossed between what is considered political and what is personal.

In every election there inevitably arises accusations of negative campaigning and who started it. A candidate may begin to use negative campaigning in their early speeches beginning with their announcement to run. They may chastise the corrupt values in government.

A newcomer may seek to discredit the incumbent and change people's perception of them, so that they will look better. They may say that the incumbent does not understand the people's problems, so it does not matter what kind of program they might have.

This approach promotes the need for change because the people cannot afford more years of a government that cannot even help its own people. A candidate may even depict their opponent as lying to the people, which can be very effective.

They might show their opponent saying things that are not considered not to be true and repeat them so often that it will lose its original meaning and become a new dramatic narrative for their opponent's broken promises.

They may ask the people to remember when their opponent said that they would be better off in four years and then ask voters how they are doing now to remind them that their opponent has made things worse for them.

Candidates often use the economy and the loss of jobs to discredit their opponent as ineffectual and not deserving of being elected. A candidate can appeal to the voter's self-interest and desire to be better off in the future, implying that any change would be better than the present to reduce uncertainty about themselves.

To counter their opponent's dramatic narratives, a candidate can characterize the incumbent as deceptive and scary, as misleading, and wanting to give tax breaks to millionaires. They may characterize their opponent as taking credit for what went right, while blaming everyone else for everything that went wrong.

Persuasive Ability

A candidate can use repetition to hammer home their message and to persuade people to vote for them.

They have to prove that change is essential by using a version of social reality characterizing the incumbent as corrupt and repugnant to persuade people to abandon their previously held beliefs.

They may use an attractive social reality to persuade people to support them. The dramatic narrative of change can be to be so persuasive it is used by most candidates. However, once in office little seems to change, so they next election candidates can again call for change.

An incumbent may use dramatic narratives of trust and experience to legitimize their candidacy. They may be initially successful in persuading people that they know how to get things done to solve their problems.

Change is the most common means of persuasion for any newcomer because if people cannot see the need for change, they are not likely to choose a new candidate over the familiarity of the incumbent. To change, people must think the current situation is more uncomfortable than taking a risk on the unknown.

In order to vote for change, people have to be motivated to want something new. Politicians do this by demonizing their opponent or utilizing a crisis. If there isn't one, a false crisis can panic people creating fear. This motivates people to vote for change because it is perceived as preferable to the status quo.

Consider how many crises have occurred before an election.

All too often politicians fail to explain what they are doing and why. They may feel that the people will just, "get it." This is a risky because people are busy.

Politicians need to be able to clearly communicate their ideas, so the public understands them because people don't necessarily just, "get it."

Campaign to Win

Chapter 6
Introducing a Candidate to The World

As an election season draws near, a candidate will began to develop their public persona and the dramatic narratives they will employ. Early in a campaign, candidates must begin to develop their own version of social reality in order to establish their legitimacy to govern.

The political challenges that face a candidate at the beginning of an election season can be legion.

In announcing their candidacy, a candidate often enters a pack of contenders. So, they will need to forge their own identity to distinguish themselves from the other candidates.

If a candidate is relatively unknown at the beginning of a campaign, they have the advantage of not having a public persona to influence the public's perception of them.

This advantage will give them leeway to craft their own public persona to appeal to as wide an audience as possible. A candidate needs to create a message that will not only hold traditional supporters, but one that would also convert enough voters to defeat their opponent's version of social reality, especially if their opponent has won past elections.

Early in the campaign, a candidate must develop a unified version of social reality consisting of many dramatic narratives that will appeal to voters.

A newcomer can appeal to voters who are dissatisfied with present conditions and want change.

This strategy alone is often not enough to win, so a candidate will have to attack and replace their opponent's dramatic narratives with their own narratives to attract moderate, independent, and opposition party voters.

In order to attract converts, a candidate must characterize the opposition's dramatic narratives as repugnant using the process of shared meaning.

Announcing Their Candidacy

In their announcement speech, a candidate begins to outline their dramatic narratives to share a new version of social reality with the public.

This version of social reality can be about facilitating change to fix the problems in government and to restore the American Dream to the people. An incumbent will focus on how their past experience can facilitate future success.

A candidate often casts themselves as the hero of the people, a public servant who is now going to make a commitment to a larger cause, often by helping the people have a better quality of life.

A candidate often refers to their accomplishments and their having traditional values like hard work, faith, family, individual responsibility, and community. Values that are under attack from their opponent.

To motivate people to support them, a candidate must characterized themselves as sharing the people's values and beliefs, which are being threatened by their opponent who is afraid to change with the rest of the world.

A candidate can undermine their opponent's legitimacy by telling people they have avoided taking responsibility, so they can provide the solutions.

The government has abandoned its own people, so now the people, must reclaim the government to move forward and solve the problems it faces.

A newcomer can say that the country has lost its way and is rapidly headed in the wrong direction. That there is a paralysis in government, which has no plan or vision for the future. There is only neglect, selfishness, and division.

The people in government have become rich because they exploited the government at the taxpayers' expense. They have been helped by the incumbent who no longer cares for the people who elected them to office in the first place.

Candidates often try to establish their legitimacy by comparing themselves to popular past Presidents like Lincoln, Truman, Roosevelt, Kennedy, or Reagan.

They characterize the differences between themselves and their opponent by using their values as a choice between neglect and restoring the values of the people.

In presenting their version of social reality, a candidate must utilize many dramatic narratives to connect with the voters. An unknown candidate must build a following through the use of shared meaning to make a connection with the voters.

They must create their version of social reality by casting their opponent and their party in the role of villains who have hurt the people and the country,

This approach is designed to share meaning with the public by separating them from their attachment to their current version of social reality to gain their support.

A newcomer must create a new version of social reality with themselves as the hero who, with the people's help, will change government to restore the American Dream. They must also undermine their opponent's legitimacy by characterizing them as the people's opponent.

A candidate's version of social reality should be well-developed developed months before their announcement to run. Then throughout the campaign, they can deploy these dramatic narratives as needed. This will help to keep them consistent, wavering little as the campaign progresses.

Dramatic narratives often connect to familiar traditions and common values. Some common narratives are about unemployment, the economy, and the people in government.

This helps them to gain support by using repetition of these narratives to create a feeling of stability and familiarity as the campaign wears on.

An Incumbent Must Begin Campaigning Early

It is common for an incumbent to wait until after the convention to begin to set out their version of social reality that will form the basis for their campaign. However, waiting so long to share meaning can cost them vital support.

If a candidate waits to communicate their version of social reality, it gives their opponent time to create and share their versions and to gain converts to their candidacy by separating people from previously shared meanings.

At the beginning of the general election, an incumbent will be faced with a different challenge from their opponent. An incumbent needs to keep the support of people who have voted for them in the past. This can be accomplished through the skillful process of sharing meaning with the people by reaffirming past dramatic narratives.

However, a candidate might have a loosely cobbled together version of social reality. This will contribute to the perception that their campaign is adrift with no discernible direction.

The media may characterize this as evidence that a candidate is struggling to find a clear message and consistent campaign strategy. Their campaign will be perceived as being adrift and left with only one consistent issue, criticizing their opponent.

An incumbent's campaign can experience difficulties beyond its control. They may be distracted by the demands of conducting the nation's business and dealing with the effects of current events.

In response to criticism of their lack of campaigning, a candidate should have a damage control strategy. They may characterize themselves as being criticized from all sides, sustaining one assault after another while they tried to do what is best for the people.

They can characterize themselves as being unfairly attacked by an opponent who has not done themselves what they are criticizing them for not doing.

In order to counter the public perception of weakness, an incumbent may say that they have chosen not to fight back until now because they believed the people want action, positive ideas, and real solutions to challenges, not just complaints. This approach utilizes the strategy of governing as a form of campaigning.

An incumbent can begin by citing the challenges they face while recalling their accomplishments. They can utilize the dramatic narrative of restoration to legitimize their campaign. An incumbent has proven their ability in the past and that experience can provide a better future under their leadership.

A candidate can build their version of social reality using restoration based on basic American principles. It can be characterized as restoring power to people, not the government.

The dramatic narrative of restoration characterizes a transference from the past to the future, identifying the economic problems and setting out their plan and guiding principles.

As there is no single cause for our problems, there is no one solution. This program is their vision of a better future and their plan for getting there.

Their plan may began with a dramatic narrative that features a golden age as a historical watershed having completed the greatest mission in the history of our country. So that they can create a vision of the future with an America restored through our most cherished principles.

An incumbent may charge that their opponent is exploiting the economy's weaknesses for political gain by creating a false perception of America in decline. In responding to criticism about the economy, they may point out that the economy is one of the best in the world.

The economy is better than their opponent wants people to believe. The critics look only at America's problems by telling the people that its best days are past.

Their response can be one of opportunity for all Americans through a reduction in the intrusion of government to provide incentives for growth.

The past has witnessed unprecedented growth and we can do this again. In this dramatic narrative, the villains are government bureaucrats who will impose unfair restrictions to hurt the economic growth.

Just as businesses downsize to stay competitive, government needs to become more streamlined to be productive. A candidate can propose cutting government staff and salaries, capping growth, and freezing spending.

Congress spends money because it gives individual members more power. Their greed knows no limits. They will spend every last dime they can squeeze from the working men and women of America.

Candidates often characterize this time in the history as a turning point for the nation. We can be a better nation through change and renewal. The government should keep taxes, interest, and regulations as low as possible to encourage growth. If capital gains are heavily taxed, it will destroy the economy.

In their program, a candidate needs to define their view of the world and create a vision of the future. They must put the public in the center of their dramatic narrative because it is the people's choice to decide which candidate fits their principles, values, and hopes for the future.

The principles of freedom that have made the United States the most dynamic society in the world are fundamental to defending the personal freedom of all Americans.

The Newcomer Version of Social Reality

To meet the challenges of the election, a candidate must create a unified social reality that they can utilize over the course of the campaign that will share meaning with the voters.

A newcomer or outsider must characterize the nation as being devastated by the present government in Washington. They can characterize the country as coming apart at the seams, deteriorating, and in serious decline. People are hurting and the government is mired in gridlock. A great nation, once respected, has become the laughing stock of the world.

Present conditions can be characterized as intolerable and the people are suffering. These problems are presented as the legacy of neglect and failed economic policies of the incumbent.

A newcomer or outsider can characterize the government as full of villains, elected officials have forgotten the people who sent them there. These people are privileged, out of touch, self-serving, and morally repugnant to the values of the people.

The American Dream, which is built on hard work, has been destroyed by a government that makes people work harder for less while rewarding speculation, privilege, and special interests.

A newcomer or outsider can characterize their opponent as lacking any leadership ability and having no program to solve the people's problems because they do not understand what the problems are. So, the people need a new leader with a new approach to solve its problems.

A newcomer or outsider should cast themselves as the hero who would bring hope to the people. Perhaps, they have grown up in humble beginnings or a small town that can be characterized as the personification of the American Dream.

They can say that they will support and protect the American Dream to give it back to the people. They will not stand by and let the next generation be the first to be worse off than their parents.

Since they are more likely to have little or no record of public service, a newcomer or outsider can cast themselves a new breed of politician and an agent of change. This can help them distance themselves from past policies to characterize themselves as a new type of politician.

Change is not only to alter the direction of the country through a new form of government, it is also a change in ideology. The people want a hard working and thoughtful leader who is concerned about the people and can get things done.

A candidate should cast themselves as a hero who when elected will make the people a priority, because they know their troubles and problems first hand and they also share their hopes and dreams.

Good, decent, and hard working people have been abandoned by their government, so they will restore fairness and economic equality to reward people who work hard and play by the rules.

The Outsider As a Servant of the People

The outsider faces a unique challenge from the other candidates. Having never served in elected office, they cannot employ many of the traditional approaches used by politicians to legitimize their candidacy like their record in office and winning past elections.

Instead, they may characterize a corrupt government that has lost its will to help the very people who elected it in the first place. The government is mired in gridlock and full of villains who wasted the people's money and mortgaged their future.

An outsider, with the help of the people, the outsider will unlock gridlock and restore the government to the people. They might characterize themselves as a humble public servant who will only take orders directly from the people and not evil special interests. In this way, the government will be returned to the people and the values of the past.

In order to develop a version of social reality, it helps to create a scene of the country in trouble that is caused by the current people in government. People are out of work and families are hurt by failed economic policies.

Washington is doing nothing to help the people or to create jobs because they have no idea what to do to help. None of these politicians have ever run a business or created any jobs. They have spent their lives in government, which is the problem not the solution.

The future of our children and grandchildren is being mortgaged by the national debt and the government does nothing about it. So, we are in danger of losing the American Dream.

Thus, an outsider can characterize Washington as full of people who came to serve, but ended up cashing in. Elected officials listen only to special interests and lobbyists rather than representing the people.

The people in Washington are characterized as corrupt. They do not know how to work together, all they knew is how to fight each other. Washington is a mess and out of touch with the people. If elected, the outsider will rid the country of the mess and corruption in Washington.

It is up to the people to correct the problems the nation faced by restoring the government without harming what is good. The dramatic narrative of restoration is used to return the government to the people. Political principles are drawn from traditional values coming from the people themselves.

An outsider can cast themselves as a personification of the American Dream. Someone who came from humble beginnings and worked hard to achieve success.

They are in this for love of country and love of its people to pass on the American Dream, that they have experienced, to our children and grandchildren.

An outsider might say that they are willing to finance their own campaign and not accept contributions. Thus, they can claim a populist mandate based on tradition common values that came from the people themselves. This makes the people an important part of their version of social reality.

Avoiding The Use of Dramatic Narratives

In contrast, if a candidate avoids the use of dramatic narratives or does not communicate a clear and attractive version of social reality, it will give their campaign the feeling of lacking any direction or coherence. Some politicians have a tendency to avoid the use of dramatic narratives to inspire or inform the people.

An incumbent will focus on the accomplishments of the past as evident that they will confront the challenges of the future. They will say that the experiences and resources gained from past successes can now be used to solve problems today.

However, an incumbent cannot easily cast the government as villains. Instead they should redefine the issue by turning it around to characterize their opposition as looking only at the problems and exploiting the people by telling them we are in decline with our best days past.

An incumbent will want to stay the course to get back to the work they started years ago. They may try to cast themselves as the real agent of change. The kind of change that matters with traditional values.

An incumbent is in a unique position to claim a popular mandate from the people because they were elected by the people.

Their announcement must also be made in a place of real significance to them or what they stand for, so it will share meaning with the voters. Where candidates announce their candidacy has great significance because it shares meaning with the public about who they are and sets the tone for their campaign.

In an announcement, an incumbent can say the reason for seeking another term is to finish the important work that they have begun. They must mention their popular mandate and their own self-sacrifice by serving the people.

They might cast themselves as a hero who will save the country from the threat posed by their opponent. They may cast themselves and the American people as heroes with a clear course of action to save the country from their opponent and their party.

An announcement speech is vital to lay the groundwork to establish a candidate as the people's chosen leader. They may use a collective 'we' or 'us' to create a shared meaning that we are all in this together.

An announcement speech must be in a location that symbolizes a candidate's campaign and represented familiar traditions like a return to their roots and the shared values that they want to restore.

All too often candidates communicate a trackless set of dramatic narratives that lack any coherent social reality. This gives an appearance of being hastily put together and the impression that their campaign is in disarray.

As the campaign season approaches, the challenge for an incumbent is to maintain their support and build on it up to the next election. They must keep those who shared their version of social reality and voted for them in the last election committed to them.

Some incumbents make the mistake of assuming this will just happen. It takes effort to keep their supporters and bring back those who no longer shared their version of social reality.

Characterization of The Issues

Most of the time it's the domestic problems that are the public's top concern like the economy, education, unemployment, health care, and the deficit. Foreign affairs often are at the bottom of the list as the least important issues of concern to voters.

Change in public perception of these issues can be affected by how well a candidate's version of social reality is shared by the public. It will also be affected by the lack of an effective version of social reality characterizing their opposition.

If a candidate cannot clearly articulate what they stand for, people will wonder why they should vote for them.

A candidate must lead the debate because a reactionary approach will by seen as a sign of weakness. All too often candidates concentrate on details and policy rather than creating any form of shared meaning with the public to communicate their version of social reality.

This approach will be perceived as poorly thought out dramatic narratives that fail to share meaning with the public. This will set a lackluster tone that will hurt them throughout the campaign.

An incumbent must hold supporters to their version of social reality, which they may find difficult to accomplish with growing opposition.

They may try a strategy of campaigning by governing, by conducting the people's business. However, this will not work and can force them into a defensive posture making them appear weak and without a plan.

A candidate must clearly articulate the reasons for voters to support their candidacy, and develop strong reasons that will undermine their opponent's legitimacy.

Chapter 7
Getting Name Recognition in The Primaries

After announcing their candidacy, a candidate is faced with a number of obstacles they will have to overcome in their bid for office.

Their biggest challenge is to carry forward and build upon the dramatic narratives introduced in their announcement.

A candidate must gain name recognition quickly to stand out in a potentially crowded field of contenders.

Early in the campaign, a candidate might accomplish this by giving a series of speeches in a place of significance to their campaign to draw together the dramatic narratives that will share meaning with the voters and help to develop their version of social reality.

These speeches are important because they outline the plan that they will utilize for the rest of the campaign. Some topics might include: economic revitalization, helping the people, change, national security, restoration, rebirth, the mess in government, and the American Dream.

A candidate will use these speeches to try to pry people loose from their previously held beliefs by casting their opposition as villains who have hurt the economy, the country, and the people. They cling to old ways of the past that no longer work in a rapidly changing world.

Their opponent must be characterized as the villain who has no vision, leadership, or strategy. So, a new approach is needed to solve our problems and restore new life to the American Dream.

A candidate may also characterize themselves as not being a typical politician, so they can begin to break up old ideas about the parties and cast themselves in a different mold.

In order to legitimize their candidacy, a candidate will use dramatic narratives to separate themselves from the evils of the government they attacked. The election is a crusade to build a better future by restoring basic values for the forgotten middle class to provide opportunity and restore the American dream.

A candidate should focus on issues where they rate low or that are the most important to voters like the economy, education, or health care. This is to improve their ratings with the public. If they only focus on areas of strength, they are less likely to gain much needed public support.

A newcomer can focus on the number of people who feel that they are worse off than a year ago, who are working hard but not getting ahead, or are worried that the next generation will be worse off than the last because upward mobility is no longer something to be taken for granted.

If poll categories begin to reflect a candidate's dramatic narratives it will suggest that they are being shared by the voters. Or, the electorate had previously shared these dramatic narratives, so a candidate should recognize this and utilize them. All too often they don't.

Primary Debates

Debates will represent one of the first tests of a candidate's campaign under fire from direct opposition. A candidate version of social reality will now face direct response and rebuttal by other candidates.

During the debates, a candidate must utilize many of the dramatic narratives developed in their announcement and subsequent speeches.

A candidate can use the debates as a forum to develop their version of social reality to demonstrate how they can help the people as an agent of change. They may compare themselves to their opponent by characterizing them as having a tepid, stay the course attitude that has got us into trouble in the first place.

We must go beyond the gridlock of the past to develop a new partnerships between the public and private sectors. Much of our present economic trouble has resulted from the government's attitude toward the people.

In contrast, we must not defend government, but rather work to improve it for the people. All people should have the chance to live up to their God given potential. We must stand up and do what is right for the people who work harder while their incomes went down and taxes went up.

A newcomer may say that they are running for office because they are fed up with being on the receiving end of the current government. This creates a broad unifying version of social reality that can energize the voters by utilizing specific dramatic narratives to support their campaign.

The Primary Campaign

Early in a campaign, an incumbent may face a serious challenge from within their own party. This may encourage the media to characterize the incumbent as being vulnerable. A contest between an incumbent and a newcomer can exposed the lack of any coherent dramatic narratives.

At first an incumbent may try to avoid attacking a member of their own party, but if their opponent's message begins to catch on with voters, they will be forced to get tough to eliminate them from the race.

They can use dramatic narratives designed to establish their credibility and answer their critics by demonstrating their concern for the issues. To connect with the people, an incumbent will need to ask the people to help them to win.

A candidate often emphasizes the economy and domestic issues. They may criticize an incumbent for their support of free trade at the expense of American workers and for having foreign lobbyists as political advisors.

A newcomer will criticize an incumbent for abandoning the values of the people and presiding over a bloated government that creates too much regulation and overspends while raising taxes.

The villains are the people in government like the incumbent who helps those abroad, while abandoning our own people here at home.

An Incumbent's Dramatic Narratives

During the primaries, an incumbent can be forced into a defensive position because they must reconstitute supporters through the process of shared meaning.

They will need to maintain the support of voters who shared their version of social reality, then they must strengthen marginal supporters, and finally bring back those who have gone to other candidates.

It is not a good plan for an incumbent to criticize the government or the economy because they have participated in creating the present situation.

An incumbent cannot use the same narratives as other candidates and if they fail to develop their own, they will appear out of touch with the country.

Should an incumbent acknowledge the problems that are being characterized by the other candidates, it will undermine their chances of being re-elected.

So, they will need to say that the country may be facing troubles, but is not falling apart as their opponents want people to believe.

An incumbent must stress their past successes as evidence that they are the best candidate.

Rather then focusing on policies and positions, an incumbent should develop a complete unified version of social reality comprised of creative dramatic narratives that will share meaning with the people.

An incumbent should focus on the positive aspects of their record and their successes. They must build on their past popularity and successes to project a vision of a better future. They need to show how they have the ability to solve difficult problems both abroad and at home.

We must look past the old ways of thinking to reform government by eliminating regulation that slows down the economy and costs jobs. Needless regulation is an evil that destroys jobs and weighs down businesses.

They may use the health care system to illustrate the differences between their program and their opponent. Health care is a convenient target because it is a problem for many people and costs too much. Even though the present system provides the best quality health care, it has its faults and should be reformed.

A candidate may create dramatic narratives depicting the struggle between building on success or adopting failure, between individual choice or government imposition. It is necessary to reduce the power of government to restore individual freedom and choice.

A Newcomer's Dramatic Narratives

A newcomer has the luxury of being able to define their campaign on their own terms. The focus of a newcomer's campaign is to describe what is wrong with the incumbent and the government.

A newcomer must criticize of the current government in power, but may not provide many specifics for change.

They may not be forthcoming with their own proposals for change and only focus on being critical of others. They are often given more time to develop their positions as the campaign unfolds.

A newcomer can play the role of the reluctant candidate. They are not seeking office for their own gain, but if the people want them, they will work for the people. An outsider may use their business experience as evidence that they can solve the country's problems.

A newcomer will likely say that they are running for office because they love their country, the people, and the principles it is founded on, and because they are tired of seeing these principles violated by their opponent.

A newcomer or outsider usually runs primarily against the incumbent rather than other candidates. Taking on the most well known candidate or the incumbent usually gets them more attention and shows that they are a serious candidate.

A newcomer or outsider can take advantage of dramatic narratives characterizing themselves as a plain speaking, straight talking, get the job done alternative to the deception and inaction in government.

A newcomer or outsider's blunt speaking style can add to their public persona of an ordinary person who is not a polished orator, but speaks the truth from the heart.

A populist, euphemistic, plain style of speaking, and ready wit is reminiscent of early rhetorical styles that are deeply rooted in the American political tradition.

Using dramatic narratives of being a plain speaking candidate of the people will share meaning with the people and the media. They may even be compared to Harry Truman who had the same qualities.

As a campaign progresses, a newcomer will began to add more specific dramatic narratives until a clear and coherent version of social reality emerges.

A newcomer should utilized the dramatic narrative of restoration by saying that they will restore the government to the people to whom it rightfully belonged.

A newcomer can also develop their version of the American Dream dramatic narrative. They may say that they want to give future generations the American Dream, which they have been fortunate enough to live. In this way, they will present a populist persona.

To share meaning with the average person, a newcomer can say that they came from humble beginnings and have been blessed with prosperity through hard work and helping others because America is the land of opportunity unlike any other nation on earth.

However, to gain support a newcomer needs to shake people loose from their old versions of social reality by characterizing their opponent and the current government as repugnant in the worst possible terms.

They must communicate a compelling reason for change to persuade voters to switch to a new and unfamiliar version of social reality. So, the new one must be made to be more appealing than the old social reality to reduce uncertainty.

To accomplish this, a newcomer can utilize dramatic narratives characterizing the people in government as villains who created the mess the country is in. The government can no longer be tolerated by the people and must be changed for the country to solve the problems it faces.

The people in government do not know how to solve the people's problems. They do not know how things work. They do not even know what the problems really are. What they do know is how to take money from lobbyists and profit for themselves.

The government should come from the people, instead it comes at the people. The country has to be put back under the control of the people who are its owners.

Politicians blame each other when they should work together to solve the country's problems. Instead, they bicker, fight, and point fingers to avoid responsibility.

Yet, they spend money at an alarming rate, creating the largest debt in history. If anyone in a business did the same things, they would go to prison.

A newcomer can characterize the tax code as unfair, made to help special interests. It should be thrown out and the government should start over.

They can characterize the government's economic policies as spending our children's and grandchildren's money to mortgage their future. It is irresponsible for the government to put this burden on them.

The government has let the job base deteriorate, creating tax users when it must help business to grow to create taxpayers. Government must stop its adversarial relationship with business and form partnerships to compete in a global economy.

Businesses must be kept strong to protect jobs and make the words 'made in the USA' a standard of excellence in the world.

Heroes and Villains

In a novel or film, a writer usually casts an individual as the hero who is pitted against another individual who is cast as the villain because it is easier for the audience to identify with an individual than an idea or policy.

A well developed dramatic narrative will feature a villain who exhibits behaviors that are contrary to the nation's basic beliefs and values. A candidate should then cast themselves as a hero who will stand up to this villain. This makes their dramatic narratives engaging and action oriented.

An incumbent's approach might be to react to attacks and address specific issues as their opponents raise them, rather than setting their own agenda. The nature of these attacks, and how they respond to them will help make them appear strong and in control or weak and under siege.

An incumbent can be forced by their opponent to move to the right or left in order to maintain their base, so their opponent can take the middle ground in a campaign. This will undermine the legitimacy and wide spread appeal they need to win and stay in office.

Chapter 8
Accusation and Refutation in The General Election

Once a candidate accepts their party's endorsement, the campaign enters a new phase. In recent times this rite of passage has become largely symbolic.

With the rise of the primary system, party conventions have little real significance. They mostly serve as free advertising for candidates to promote themselves and bash their opposition.

From the conventions to Election Day, the two major party candidates focus on one another in their quest for office. During this time, they will employ dramatic narratives to establish themselves as having the legitimate right to govern, while trying to undermine their opponent's legitimacy.

Ideally, an election campaign provides voters the information necessary to cast an informed and thoughtful vote based on the issues.

However, it is more likely that the candidate who can scare the most people into fearing their opponent, will motivate enough people to vote for them to win.

Due to the adversarial nature of the American political system, the general election is often a time of accusation and refutation.

There is a tendency for a candidate to grow more strident and negative to galvanize their supporters and shake loose those who share their opponent's version of social reality.

Negative campaigning, dirty politics, and mudslinging with candidates exchanging charges and counter charges are encouraged by the media who often share these dramatic narratives because they have a tendency to view them as 'newsworthy.'

The proportion of logic and evidence diminishes during the general election as more emotional dramatic appeals, usually in the form of television commercials increases. This tendency towards television ads enhances the potential attractiveness of the use of dramatic narratives.

The political television commercial is often a short dramatic narrative filled with actors in a melodramatic format that casts a heroic persona who represents good that is pitted against the villainous persona of the opposition candidate.

It is these shared dramatic narratives that become the major battle ground in the approaching final days of the campaign.

It is often the case that a rational argument is relatively ineffective when used against previously shared dramatic narratives.

A dramatic narrative that is widely shared by the public is unlikely to be stopped with reason or explanation.

In order to attack a shared dramatic narrative, a candidate might use the same facts or events, but interpret them in a new or different way.

They may turn the dramatic narrative against their opponent with a turn of phrase or reinterpretation of the same events. Or they may create a new dramatic narrative to divert public attention in a different direction.

This chapter examines how the exchanges between the candidates in their speeches and television commercials between the conventions and Election Day.

During this time, candidates select and adapted their version of social reality to undermine their opponent's legitimacy and bolster their own.

After winning their party's nomination, a candidate should waste very little time in beginning their campaign. At the onset of the general election campaign, a candidate can use the advantage of a post convention bounce.

History suggests that this lead will dissipate over time, so a candidate's challenge is to galvanize the support they gain as quickly as possible.

A candidate might say that the test of leadership involves understanding how the world has changed, how to assert our role in the world, and to summon the people's values, economic and military strengths to support their new vision.

A newcomer might characterize the incumbent as having failed to meet these new challenges because they hold on to old assumptions and policies that maintain the status quo.

The incumbent's foreign policy is designed for old ways of thinking and does not fit the new challenges of a changing world.

A newcomer may accuse an incumbent of failing to stand up for our values and ignoring human rights atrocities in other countries. They might call their opponent's claim of changing the world being as flawed as their contention of changing things at home. They let opportunity slip by instead of reaching out to embrace it.

A newcomer may attack an incumbent's biggest success by recasting history saying that it is the incumbent who has created the problem they claim to have solved in the first place.

The incumbent would rather talk about their past accomplishments when this should not be the measure of leadership. Leadership is about opportunities seized and crises adverted.

Leadership is about being strategic, vigorous, and grounded in America's values rather than their opponent who is reactive and tied to a status quo that failed.

By doing this, a newcomer can take the familiar dramatic narratives of an incumbent and attach new characterizations to them in order to support their candidacy.

The incumbent can be cast as opposing traditional American values. Unlike the incumbent, the newcomer will stand up for the American values of democracy and freedom by working for human rights and standing against aggression.

In order to promote our national interests, a candidate should promote the growth of democracies abroad because they provide stable trading partners and rarely create military threats.

A candidate should be concerned with how other countries govern their people by making human rights a primary consideration in foreign policy decisions, because foreign policy cannot be divorced from our moral principles.

In creating a dramatic narrative linking foreign policy to domestic policy, a newcomer has two objectives. First, to blunt criticism of the lack of foreign policy experience by characterizing such experience as not important. Second, to make success in foreign policy contingent on success at home.

A candidate's first priority should be the domestic agenda because it is important to improve the economy first. America must be strong at home in order to be strong abroad.

Focus On The People

A candidate must focus on domestic and economic problems, their cause, and their solutions. It is critical for a candidate to constantly reiterated their version of social reality by utilizing dramatic narratives that are a mainstay of their campaign from the beginning.

Utilizing the dramatic narrative of change, a candidate can affirm their belief that tomorrow can be better than today. A newcomer might characterize their plan as new and different, neither Republican nor Democrat, neither liberal nor conservative. Instead, they will cast themselves as an independent interested in change.

This is the charting of a new course for the nation in a radically new direction. They might make the case that their party has changed and they reject the failed economic theories of trickle down or tax and spend with big government offering a program for every problem.

Not only can the dramatic narrative of change apply to a candidate's plan to change government and the nation, it also can apply to their party and even to the candidate themselves.

Using this approach, a candidate can characterize the old dramatic narratives of the past administration as the source of the nation's problems. This supports their need for change.

As a part of the rationale for change, a candidate can accuse their opponent of promising growth, tax cuts, and debt reduction, but instead left inequality, economic decline, and the nation in debt.

Instead, they brought deficits, slow growth, tax burdens, and a decline in productivity. These promises are hollow because they betrayed the people's trust.

A candidate should try to redefine their opponent's well-know statements by reinterpreting them from their original meaning as proof that they are dishonest.

They might characterize their opponent as being self-centered, caring only about winning the election rather than serving the people. They did not help average working people who makes less and pays more. Instead they make things worse because they have no programs to help the people or solve their problems.

A New Characterization of a Candidate

Candidates often exploit the differences between themselves and their opponent. They may claim that their opponent constantly changes their mind on every issue. The people are deserving of better treatment than they have received from their government.

Pessimists, like their opponent take unfair advantage of the economy and have attacked them while they are trying to get things done for the people. They can characterize the country as coming out of tough times, but not to believe the pessimists who tear the country down.

They can accuse their opponent as turning the campaign negative when the people want a positive debate of the issues. This will help to separate their opponent from the values of the people whom they want to serve.

A candidate can accuse their opponent of playing the tired old game politicians use to pit the rich against the poor by using divisiveness to further their campaign through class warfare.

They talk a lot, but do nothing. When the people hear them, remember their record because their actions betray their words. The people deserve better and can do better to confront the challenges it faces. The people should have a feeling of optimism for the country, to rise above today's conditions to achieve a better tomorrow.

A candidate must ask for the people's support as part of their version of social reality. An election is like interviewing for a job. The people must know who they are, their record, their strengths, and their mistakes.

When people are asked what is the most important problem facing the country, the majority said economic issues, however, they are often unclear about what specific economic issues they mean. Unemployment, cost of living, inflation, the trade deficit, and recession or depression are often the most common.

In the past, when people expressed a concern over the economy they usually cited a specific issue such as unemployment, the deficit, or inflation.

More recently, people who have a concern for the economy gave few details, suggesting that dramatic narratives are being shared that criticized the economy with few specifics.

The Great Conversion

At some point in the election, often well before Election Day, enough people will have made up their mind to determine the election's outcome. After this, the bulk of campaigning will make little difference.

This point in the campaign is The Great Conversion, especially if public sentiment has shifted over the course of the campaign or against a popular incumbent.

The purpose of a campaign is to reduce uncertainty about a candidate, while increasing uncertainty about their opponent. This happens when a candidate attacks their opponent's dramatic narratives that have previously shared meaning with the voters.

At first, a candidate may have limited success against their opponent, but may have little effect in eroding their support. Eventually, an incumbent's version of social reality will come under attack from their opponent.

If a newcomer's dramatic narratives become more widely shared by the people, they will began to express their discontent with the incumbent.

If the incumbent comes under attack, but does not adequately defend themselves while their opponent relentlessly hammers away at them, they will lose support. Public perception of the incumbent will become more like their opponent's characterization of them.

If a candidate is successful in recasting their opponent's dramatic narratives, a major block of the electorate can be separated from their old version of social reality. One indication of this occurring is the emergence of a high percentage of angry voters. This is a typical reaction to the process of changing social reality.

While shifting from a previously held social reality to a new one, people may feel angry or confused. Polls may show an increase in angry voters. This happens when a significant portion of the people express anger with the government and dissatisfaction with the candidates.

If the voters are unhappy with the incumbent, it would seem that they would simply change allegiances and support another candidate.

However, many will want another candidate to enter the race or will support an outsider. This shows that a majority of the people are searching for another version of social reality.

When the people become dissatisfied with their old version of social reality, it will be shown in the incumbent's rising disapproval ratings.

The media may reflect a characterization of the incumbent as not running a strong campaign and lacking conviction on the issues. They might characterize the incumbent as being uncertain about their campaign and the direction it should take.

When a newcomer or outsider enters the race they will attack the establishment candidate's social reality to get their supporters to switch to their own dramatic narratives.

During this time some voters will be looking for another version of social reality. They would likely find the newcomers version attractive to them. This explains why an outsider can achieve an unusually high level of support.

If the incumbent's campaign is in disarray or there is no one to defend their version of social reality, it is unlikely that voters will support an incumbent's version of social reality in any significant numbers.

A shift in public opinion can leave voters separated from their old version of social reality and searching for a new one. Although a few may return to their previously shared version of social reality, an overwhelming number are likely to support a new one.

If the core support, that is those people who would not consider another candidate, for a newcomers is above that of the incumbent, the conversion of social reality has taken place.

Even though public opinion suggests that many of the issues a candidate employs exists before the campaign begins, a newcomer can effectively exploit them by panicking people into believing that the state of the country is so bad that something drastic has to be done to avert a total crisis.

The inability of an incumbent to recapture voters' support would seem to show the significance of a conversion to a new version of social reality.

If an incumbent is unable to regain those who have lost their version of social reality in any significant numbers, they will not be re-elected.

When a candidate's public image turns negative, the conversion to a new version of social reality has likely run its course. If the number of angry voters begins to subside, this shows that the conversion to another version of social reality has stabilized.

Chapter 9
Closing the Deal, The Race to Election Day

In developing their version of social reality, a newcomer can utilize dramatic narratives about the American people casting the people as heroes, as good people who have figured out that there is something wrong with the government, so it needs to be changed.

A newcomer must characterize the government as mired in gridlock and their opponent as a villain who came to serve the people, but instead made excuses and cashed in for themselves.

They answer to special interests and lobbyists instead of the people. Washington attracts ego driven, power mad people, when it should attract the best qualified to serve.

After setting up the negative characteristics of their opponent, a newcomer can compare them on specific issues. Like, the people know it is wrong to spend our children's money, yet the government will pass on a huge debt to them.

The people want the government to rebuild and reorganize the job and industrial base, keep industry from going abroad, put people back to work, and make the words made in the USA the world's standard for excellence.

An incumbent's dramatic narratives will usually focus on characterizing themselves as having demonstrated the ability to govern. They will say that they are the only candidate who can be trusted and who has the experience to govern.

They will focus on the difference between themselves and their opponent, their records in office, and their plans for the future.

If a candidate wants to characterize their opponent as a liberal, they will likely use the dramatic narrative of tax and spend to cast them as a villain who supports high taxes and government programs that wastes the people's money.

To pay for their increased spending, they will increase taxes not just on the rich, but also on the middle class and working poor.

In order to get votes, candidates often promise to increase spending, often by billions of dollars. But the people must reject candidates who have a record of being a tax and spend liberal.

They must characterize their opponent as having been dishonest in the past, so the people cannot trust them in the future.

They may characterize their opponent as taking both sides of important issues, never making their position clear. This utilizes the dramatic narratives of trust, credibility, and honesty, to demonstrate that their opponent is unfit for office to undermine their legitimacy.

Another way a candidate can exploit their opponent's unfitness for office is to show specific examples of tax raises their plan will cause.

They say that they will only tax the rich to pay for their campaign promises, however, reputable economists say their plan means higher taxes for everyone and bigger deficits.

This issue can be made more personal by showing specific people and estimating how much their taxes will increase under their opponent's plan. This is done to discredit an opponent's plan and cast them as deceptive, as well as a liberal tax and spend politician.

The people cannot trust their economic plan because it is wrong for them and wrong for America. Thus, a dramatic narrative is created of their dishonest opponent whose programs would make things worse for ordinary people.

Rapid Response Team

It is helpful for a candidate to have a rapid response team to reply to their opponent's charges. Slow responses to attacks by an opponent will give the appearance of weakness or an admission of guilt.

By responding to an opponent's charges quickly, a candidate can create the impression of being unfairly attacked and competent enough to deal with these situations.

Negative ads and personal attacks can be characterized as not only an attack on the candidate, it is also an attack on the American people because they only want to help the people. Any distraction or attack on a candidate prevents the people's problems from being solved.

Whenever attacked, a candidate needs to be quick to answer. They may try to recast their dramatic narratives to bolster their legitimacy and undermine their opponent's. They may even go further to attack the legitimacy of their opponent with a direct reference to their dramatic narratives.

A candidate may respond by saying that they will institute a new approach to reinvent government that is neither liberal nor conservative, neither Democratic nor Republican to help them claim a popular mandate for change as a representative of the people. This can help them to escape past negative connotations that will hurt their campaign.

However, rather than simply outlining their policies and programs, a series of dramatic narratives can cast the past as having damaged the country by violating the people's and the nation's values. The government betrayed the values that made America great.

These dramatic narratives are designed to separate people from their current version of social reality by characterizing it as repugnant, so they must change.

People who shared meaning with the current version of social reality are now told that their beliefs are wrong, because the government has betrayed the people, so it must stop.

A candidate will help them to fix their problems, to provide opportunity to give every American hope for the future. This can make their version of social reality as appealing as possible by casting it in the best possible terms.

This approach is designed to change public perception, so a candidate can then cast their attackers as villains who have divided the people against each other pitting rich against poor, black against white, women against men.

A candidate can then cast themselves as the hero who will save the people, put America back to work, and help them prosper. America needs a new approach that will give new hope to the people and breathe new life into the American dream.

A candidate might add other dramatic narratives about the nature of government and a political system that isn't working. Instead, it is dominated by powerful interests, and an entrenched bureaucracy.

A New Kind Of Politician

In order to develop a new version of social reality, a candidate can characterize themselves as a new type of politician. They are a part of a new generation that doesn't think the way the old politicians do

This approach serves to separate them from the old dramatic narratives of liberal or conservative by saying that they have rejected the old style politics.

Without being too specific, they can claim that they differ from politicians of the past. This dramatic narrative characterizes a departure from what is typically perceived as old and failed programs of the past.

This approach is designed to neutralize an opponent's accusation that characterizes them as a politics as usual candidate.

If a candidate wants to characterize themselves as an experienced leader, they may use ads to create persuasive messages. They can be shown sitting behind a desk in an office with the American and state flags behind them. They could also be shown still working, late at night with their suit jacket off and sleeves rolled up to show them being thoughtfully engaged in the people's business.

They can establish their credibility by marshaling an array of endorsements like Nobel Prize winners, respected business leaders, independent experts, and even people who have previously supported their opponent. They must demonstrate their program as the best hope for reviving the economy to get the country moving again.

They need to counter their opponent's criticisms of their program as being detrimental for the people and the nation. Since so many successful people and experts backed them, their credibility should be used to transfer to them legitimizing their candidacy.

People and Crowds

Another approach to legitimize a candidate is to show them campaigning along with images of people. They will be seen as popular when shown speaking to large rallies, on a bus tour route, or with crowds of cheering people waving flags. This scene depicts a candidate of the people who is in touch with the average person and understands their problems.

These scenes of a candidate mingling with the people characterizes them as one of the people. A candidate can also be shown with their sleeves rolled up, as if they are ready to go to work. Showing them with veterans, law enforcement, or military personnel is designed to portray them as a strong candidate.

A candidate must be shown speaking to crowds at outdoor rallies, then talking to individual people, and being surrounded by a crowd of exuberant people waving flags and their campaign signs. These scenes visually reinforce the dramatic narrative of having the support of the people.

These familiar narratives of change and the people are supported with visual images that capture their spirit. These commercials put a candidate in the center of their own dramatic narratives as a the hero who will help the people and be a catalyst for change.

The kind of change that would improve the lives of people who are currently forgotten by their government and who would come first if they are elected. These are people with whom they have personal contact and understood.

A Candidate As a Creature of the Media

A candidate's public image can become a creature of the media. Candidates must make effective use of national television to gain public support for their candidacy.

Candidate often run the bulk of their campaign using television, supported by more traditional political rallies and stump speeches.

By using an innovative combination of new social media and traditional methods, they can communicate to the American people about issues they feel are important to the country.

In order to establish their legitimacy as a serious candidate, a newcomer has to present their view of the problems facing the country and their plan to fix those problems. They have to demonstrate the ability to accomplish these tasks and that they have a popular mandate to support themselves and their plan.

A newcomer can characterize their program as keeping the American people informed to make intelligent decisions as owners of this country. Democrats and Republicans blame one another, so nobody steps up to the plate and accepts responsibility for anything.

These issues can be a part of a candidate's plan for a new America as a country restored. America can be purposeful and thriving, a place where people work hard, not look for work. Where people save, not spend what they earn.

As the basis of their call for change, a newcomer may characterize the state of the country where America has become a violent, crime ridden society, with an ineffective school system.

We are losing our standard of living, because more children now live in poverty. The children are our hopes and dreams so we need to do it for them and for the future.

The nation has to learn to balance its budget like ordinary people have to balance theirs. The tax system should be discarded, so that we can have a new and fair system.

The other candidates sold out the American people by sending jobs overseas. Instead of coming to serve they cashed in. So, we must leave the American Dream of a better life to future generations.

In order to share meaning with the people, a newcomer can use the dramatic narrative of restoration to characterize their plan as the solution to the nation's problems.

They can also identify traditional values as part of what made our nation great and our falling away from them is the source of our recent problems.

The people need a candidate who can restore the meaning of made in the USA. Who will restore honesty, integrity, and responsibility to our government.

In this election, we have the opportunity to choose a candidate who is not a career politician, but a proven business leader with the ability to take on the tasks at hand, to balance the budget, to expand the tax base, to give our children back the American dream.

An Outsider and Business Experience

The solution to solving the people's problems in to not elect a career politician, but to elect a candidate who has proven business experience. Not a business as usual politician, but someone who can get the job done.

An outsider can use dramatic narratives of business experience, popular support, and a desire to take back their government. They can be more selective about their campaign strategy because they can have the advantage of seeing what has worked for other candidates, so they can use the positive elements of other campaigns, while avoiding negative ones.

A newcomer can utilize dramatic narratives that rate high with voters like the economy, job creation, education, and the mess in Washington, while avoiding low rated issues like foreign policy and family values.

A newcomer can criticize the government and the falling away from traditional values, which often means the incumbent without having to specifically mention them. By using this approach a newcomer can utilize negative campaigning without having to resort to the mudslinging tactics they condemn.

In order to share meaning with the voters and establish their legitimacy, a newcomer can develop the dramatic narratives of restoration, the American Dream, and being a candidate of the people.

By using television programs, a candidate can characterize their personal life and experience to establish their legitimacy through a popular mandate based on their leadership ability.

A candidate's support and qualifications can be characterized through testimonials, stories told by the people who know them. This includes personal stories of friends, family, business associates, and ordinary people by using events in their lives to demonstrate their values are traditional values.

A candidate's version of social reality can use dramatic narratives about their character and abilities. If they don't, there may be the perception in the media that they have little or no chance of winning.

A newcomer often uses dramatic narratives with themselves as the central figure or hero, who along with the American people will solve the problems facing the country. This serves to share meaning with the people because they are in this together.

The Wasted Vote

An outsider is more likely to develop a dramatic narrative that characterizes a vote for the incumbent as a vote for politics as usual, which is really a wasted vote.

They may include several villains in their dramatic narratives that include the media, the polls, and the political parties because these groups are telling people how they should vote. They might also use a dramatic narrative of their campaign under siege to galvanize their supporters.

The dramatic narrative of the wasted vote can be very useful to motivate support. If people let the media or polls tell them how to vote and do not follow their heart, then their vote will be wasted.

An election is not about voting for the winner, but about voting for what is right. If enough people feel that way, the election can turn around.

By voting for their opponents, people would be voting for politics as usual. A vote for the opponent would support things as they were, things that are getting worse.

This approach ties into the dramatic narrative of change since the other candidates represent politics as usual, so only a newcomer can effect real change.

A candidate should characterize themselves as a good and honest person who loves their country and has old fashioned values. They are a person who listens to the people and speaks from the heart.

A newcomer can urge voters to purge what is evil to restore what is good. A newcomer and the people represent the means by which restoration will take place.

A newcomer can bolster their legitimacy by connecting with the values of the people and denouncing their opponents who are not addressing the issues that are important to the people or the problems facing them.

Using Outside Sources

In the closing days of a campaign, a candidate will often use television commercials to refute their opponent's claims including attacks on their record in office. Television commercials that are attack ads generally do not feature the candidates themselves.

Credibility is often established by citing sources like news reports, television, magazines, websites, and newspapers that characterize an opponent as misleading and wrong.

Candidates often utilize sources outside themselves that the public feels is credible, so that their credibility will transfer to them.

The media is often used to attack an opponent because they give it the appearance of being objective and not coming from the candidate themselves.

A commercial may use comments from ordinary people to criticize an opponent. They may question their honesty. They may say that they don't trust them or they are not honorable because they say one thing and do something else. They may exploit the public's fear of change by saying that they scare or worry them.

When a Campaign Comes Crashing Down

If a candidate does little to develop an early version of social reality, or rely on previously shared dramatic narratives left over from the past, they will lose support.

If a candidate's campaigning is primarily reactionary responding to attacks rather than presenting any of their own initiatives, they will lose.

The all too common strategy of reacting to attacks and poll data after the fact, instead of developing their own version of social reality, will set the norm for a campaign in which a candidate will rarely, if ever lead the political debate.

If a candidate sets the agenda early on for their campaign they are much more likely to win. When they are besieged personal attacks, they must stay the course by repeatedly returning to their original version of social reality.

This strategy of creating and inculcating action based dramatic narratives to share meaning with the voters should save their campaign, especially if their credibility is low and later when their opponents attack their legitimacy.

On the other hand, if a candidate develops no coherent version of social reality of their own at the beginning of the campaign, they are more likely to lose because they have nothing to fall back on when the campaign gets tough.

A lack of focus and constant changes in a campaign create the perception that a campaign is in disarray and that a candidate has no real plan for the country. This perception will prove to be a liability that will picked up by the media and the public throughout the campaign.

A newcomer can demonstrate the power of how a candidate can share meaning with the public by employing several familiar dramatic narratives even while having few, if any, real positions on the issues. Artistically crafted dramatic narratives that share meaning with the voters will help them in the polls.

The skillful use of dramatic narratives demonstrates how a political novice, with little party support can capture the imagination of the people. Insight into how this happened can be found in how each candidate constructs their respective version of social reality.

Political Parties and Campaign Donors

There can be an aversion to candidates who seek political power for their own designs, but a candidate must clearly say that they want to be elected to office because all too often it is only implied.

Political parties and campaign donors should require candidates to be able to clearly articulate their version of social reality utilizing dramatic narratives that will share meaning with the voters before getting their support.

No candidate should run out of convenience, duty, to help their resume, to get a book deal, to increase their speaking fees, to get attention, to further a cause, to bolster or repair their public image, because it's their turn, because they are the incumbent, or to fulfill other people's expectations.

A candidate should run because they want the job and will campaign to the best of their ability to get it.

Chapter 10
Using The Power of Social Reality to Win

In order to get elected, candidates must create and share their version of social reality with the voters.

Social reality is how people make sense of the world around them. It is how we organize and make sense of our experiences, perceptions and expectations. Candidates can utilize this process by characterizing events in a manner that helps them get elected.

Social reality is important because it affects how we interpret our perceptions and determines what we do about them, so it can have tangible consequences.

A candidate's version of social reality is usually comprised of selected portions of the larger societal social reality.

It gives a particular interpretation of events with the purpose of legitimizing the candidate and undermining their opponent. It has to be compatible with the larger societal view of social reality in order to be accepted by the public.

If not, a candidate may be perceived as too extreme or out of touch with the people. These specialized versions of social reality can fall into generally accepted categories that often have a specific name like conservative, moderate, or liberal, but can be given their own set of unique characteristics.

A Newcomer's Version of Social Reality

A newcomer's version of social reality should center on a characterization of government as corrupt and the nation as coming apart at the seams. Their characterizations of the government are likely to be widely shared as evidenced by the influence of the angry voter.

Since an incumbent inherits the current, and perhaps the previous regime's legacy, a newcomer needs to characterize the current government as having hurt the people by characterizing them as full of greed and corruption.

Instead of being the restorers of American greatness, the previous regime are its destroyers. In essence, a newcomer is running not only against the incumbent, but against the legacy of previous regimes of the same party.

The vilification of the incumbent and the government is a very effective dramatic narrative that can be widely shared with the public and the media.

In order to get people to change, it has to be made attractive to them, so a newcomer has to increase public dissatisfaction and uncertainty in the current government, while reducing uncertainty about themselves.

If the level of public uncertainty about a newcomer is higher than the incumbent, they would likely lose. If it is higher about the incumbent, the newcomer will benefit.

So, an outsider's characterization of their vision of the future not only has to be perceived as being better than the present, it also has to be perceived as safe and nonthreatening to reassure the voters that their leadership is not risky.

To do this, a newcomer or outsider should use dramatic narratives of themselves as a new kind of politician who has the ability to solve their problems and public skepticism of them should begin to fade.

A candidate's version of change can also include a change in leadership, a change in their party, and a change in the country.

Change is not only about changing the direction of the country, but also about a changing people's social reality.

In order to present themselves as a new breed of politician and an agent of change, a candidate can distance themselves from the dramatic narratives of the past that can hurt the public's faith in their legitimacy for office.

Calling themselves a new type of politician, a candidate can characterize themselves as a new kind of moderate leader who rejects old style political labels like tax and spend big government liberal.

If their program is given a new name and if it sounds new to the people, it would not conjure up past negative dramatic narratives.

Creating new dramatic narratives helps to remove past negative connotations that the voters might react against. So, when their opponent calls them a tax and spend liberal or elitist conservative, a candidate can simply reject the label allowing them to also attack these policies as a failure.

In doing so, a candidate is able to selectively take credit for successes, while demonstrating that they have experienced the evils of government, so they can claim a common experience with the people.

A Candidate's Version of Social Reality

If a candidate's version of social reality is not distinct or well-defined, or if it changes throughout the campaign, it will give the people the perception that they have no plan and that their campaign is in disarray.

If a candidate is caught without a plan, when they are attacked by their opponent, they will be seen as being out of touch with the people. This will let the other candidate define them and set the agenda for the campaign. When they finally do campaign, they will likely appear reactionary and in trouble.

Many of the dramatic narratives used against candidates in the primaries that shared meaning with the voters can easily be picked up by their opposition in the general election. Coming from a member of their own party, these attacks have the effect of establishing and legitimizing many of the dramatic narratives that other candidates later used to undermine them.

This can make a previously strong candidate appear to be a weak candidate unfit for office, because now they are under siege from a faction in their own party, which should have been supporting them.

An incumbent may have to face the burden of being attacked by every candidate in the race, even from their own party, some of whom only attacked them and no other candidate.

However, an incumbent might chose a different target to legitimize their past performance by characterizing an opponent who is not an individual person or a candidate running for office in the campaign as the villain who has hurt the people. The public will find it difficult to share meaning with this is a dramatic narrative.

In any drama, like a book or movie, the hero fights an individual who is cast as the villain, not a group of undefined people who are not individually mentioned.

Throughout the primary campaign, if the incumbent presents an indistinct characterization of themselves, including who they are, and what they stand for, they will not share meaning with the voters.

While they may have the blessings of their party and the sanctifying agent of incumbency, if they do not effectively utilize this populist mandate it will not help to legitimize their claim to office.

This strategy is not effective because the lack of any version of social reality will encourage characterizations of them being weak and their campaign being disorganized without a message. These characterizations, combined with their opponent's attacks, will likely hurt their chances of winning.

An incumbent's version of social reality has to convince voters that they have the experience to solve the people's problems, but they also must convince them that this matters. Some dramatic narratives can be received negatively in the media and is not shared with the people as a significant issue in the campaign.

An incumbent may characterize how they have concentrated on running the government and waiting to run until the election is fully underway. But by then enough people have made up their mind making the race all but over.

If a candidate raises the issue of their opponent's character and judgment to undermine their legitimacy, they must do so early in the campaign. Even if a candidate is plagued by serious doubts over their credibility for most of the campaign, as the race progresses if their opponent does not bring it up early enough, the perception of their character may improve.

Since an incumbent employs many dramatic narratives about their own experience, their opponent's delegitimizing dramas about them are designed to lower the public's approval of their ability.

Incumbency is often implied, if not stressed in the issue of who would best handle a crisis. This approach promotes the value of an incumbent's experience and exposes a newcomer's weaknesses by exploiting the people's fear of the uncertainty of change.

If a newcomer is elected, who knows what might happen, but by voting for the incumbent the people know what to expect.

Some incumbents seemed to think the implication is clear and the people will get it. The voters will make the right decision to stay with an experienced incumbent because they are already in office, rather than vote for an untrustworthy, unknown, inexperienced, newcomer.

The incumbent has chosen a very risky strategy, because the people may not get it, and elect the newcomer instead.

When The Incumbent Calls For Change

While other candidates are calling to change the mess in government, an incumbent cannot call for change or criticize the failures of government. This makes their position untenable, so they may try to characterize themselves as the agent of change.

This is an impossible dramatic narrative to share meaning for the voters to share because an incumbent has been a part of the government, so they cannot easily distance themselves from it and the state of the country.

When an incumbent calls for change, it is likely to be perceived as an admission of the failure of their policies. To overcome this problem, they may characterize the villain and their primary opponent as the system, the government, or the bureaucracy, rather than another candidate.

If they take this approach, an incumbent has in effect made a tactical miscalculation and in essence validated their opponent's claim that change is really necessary.

If a candidate holds back from campaigning for too long, they will let their opponent define them and set the agenda for the campaign.

Changing Versions of Social Reality

In order to legitimize their candidacy, a newcomer needs to make a convincing case for change so that voters will be persuaded to switch their support from past versions of social reality to vote against the incumbent without supporting another candidate.

In order to do this, a candidate can employ the persuasive dramatic narratives. First, they can make the case of an intolerable situation in government in which the incumbent is ruining the country and hurting the people.

However, they might run the risk of persuading voters to leave the incumbent, but not enough to convince the people to support them, so they would end up helping another candidate instead.

Second, after they have demonstrated the need to be involved in the campaign, they presented a solution by characterizing themselves as the man of the people who can get the job done.

In order to persuade the people of the need for change, the government must be characterized as unresponsive to the people while politicians refuse to address important issues.

This dramatic narrative calls attention to the problems that must be solved. This is the motivation for a candidate's claim to office. It is the motivation for everything they do in the campaign and the basis of their version of social reality.

The task for any newcomer is to establish their legitimacy and to distinguish themselves from the other candidates as the only person who can solve the people's problems. They can accomplish this by communicating their vision of a better future, even if it is unclear what sort of future they want to create.

In order to do this, a candidate can develop the dramatic narrative of being one of the people and cast themselves as the logical candidate to provide the solutions to the people's problems.

They must cast themselves as the hero, fighting for the people against the villainous incumbent to clean up the mess in government.

The proof of their ability to govern is based on their dramatic narratives of being a success in business, a parent and family man or woman, a citizen devoted to their country, and the can-do kind of person who can get the job done no matter what the odds.

The primary legitimizing agent for them can come from popular support, so they can claim they have been sanctified by the people who want them to run.

How to Use Social Reality

In any society there is a larger overriding social reality that is shared by the people into which a candidate must fit their own version of social reality. This includes an overriding set of dramatic narratives that forms a nation's social reality.

Candidates utilize social reality in order to create their own dramatic narratives, so that they can more easily share meaning with the voters. The nature of social reality and dramatic narratives utilized in political campaigns can have larger ramifications for society.

People create dramatic narratives that tell people what is valued, what is important, and how to make sense of events. How a society interprets social reality through shared meaning can determine how successful it can become.

The media is the primary means by which we communicate dramatic narratives in society including entertainment, news, and politics. This is important because it tells us about how we perceive ourselves and what we value.

For instance, if people are constantly told that the economy is bad, they may come to believe it whether or not it is actually true. They may even act in ways to make it worse. This is how social reality becomes actual reality.

Instead of people perceiving reality as it is, their shared meanings can motivate behavior to make their perception a reality. How we as a society come to perceive things like right and wrong is often socially constructed.

The Fracturing of Social Reality

When a group's social reality is challenged either externally or internally, it may change to accommodate the new circumstances or it can fracture resulting in the creation of two competing versions of social reality. Both of these events can occur during a campaign.

When it comes under pressure, a candidate's version of social reality can change to accommodate their characterization of themselves as a new kind of politician.

If a candidate moves to the center, a wing of the party should not splinter off, attack them, or support another candidate. They must support them to win the election.

In the case of some candidates, the opposite sometimes occurs. An opponent of the same party can splinter their version of social reality early on during the primaries by publicly concentrating on selective issues creating dissatisfaction with party supporters that fractures party support.

This can push a candidate to be more extreme allowing their opponent to take the middle ground when they should cast themselves as a moderate. Many of their supporters may become dissatisfied and switch to another candidate, or sit out the election.

This will be the beginning of the end for them.

Why Ideology Shouldn't Matter So Much

When a political party has a faction that wants candidates who fit their ideology or they won't support them, it virtually ensures their defeat.

It's better to win with a candidate of your own party who has widespread public appeal and shares some of your values than to stick to your ideology and lose to a candidate who shares few or none of them.

Ideology conflicts can be resolved once in office, rather than in public during the election alienating voters and making the party appear divided.

While ideology is important to communicate what a party or candidate stands for, it can potentially alienate more voters than it attracts. Parties can get into fights over ideology that splits the party motivating people to vote against them and vote for their opponent.

What is more effective is winning elections first, and then governing.

If you lose, you can't govern or implement your policies. Once you win, ideology and policy can be worked out in the process of governing keeping it separate from campaigning.

To be successful, political parties need to put finding a candidate who can win over finding the perfect candidate who appeals to a specific faction and their ideology, because no candidate can appeal to everyone.

It is better for a party to support an imperfect candidate and win than to holdout for ideology and loose.

After all, if you are hungry, isn't it better to get half a loaf of bread than no loaf at all?

Govern to Win

Chapter 11
Campaign Like a Democrat, Govern Like a Republican

After an election, a president, or any other elected official, must form a new version of social reality that is inclusive of all the people, especially those who voted against them.

This new social reality serves to bring people together and reduce uncertainty, so the public can have confidence in their leaders and the government.

This helps a candidate make the transformation from a candidate to become a leader. Failure to do so can result in political divisions not healing.

This transformation is the process of political development that will further a politician's career. It begins with a candidate who must create uncertainty about their opponent by being divisive and negative.

After they are elected, they need to make the transformation to become a leader. This involves working with people including members of the other party.

They must exhibit leadership qualities, which includes being able to build consensus to get things done. After serving in office for many years, they may be considered a statesman, which is a politician who puts the good of the nation and the people above political considerations, even above their own interests.

For a candidate who ran on change, some politicians seem reluctant to change after being elected. Instead of legitimizing their candidacy by governing, they may continue to utilize campaign style dramatic narratives that have brought them electoral success to support their version of social reality.

Continuing to utilize campaign techniques as a means of governing after an election can serve to maintain a version of social reality that excludes some of the electorate maintaining the divisiveness of the campaign, inhibiting the larger social reality from unifying the nation.

Doing this maintains a culture of the never-ending campaign and a culture of divisiveness that is prevalent in politics and society today.

Governing and campaigning are very different processes.

An election campaign can be seen as a series of persuasive attempts by both sides to undermine their opponent's legitimacy, while bolstering their own. Candidates often draw upon forces recognized by the people including traditions, values, beliefs, and popular mandates.

As part of a campaign, candidates create and communicate dramatic narratives in order to make a connection to share meaning with the people.

The process of shared meaning is essential to a campaign because it is how a candidate motivates voters not only to vote, but also to support them by campaigning, donating money, or volunteering for them.

Sharing meaning is a powerful process because it has the potential to change perceptions and expectations, as well as motivate behavior.

Candidates often utilize established dramatic narratives because the people are familiar with them. This helps to make a candidate's version of social reality more easily understood since these dramatic narratives are ones that the people already know.

Candidates need to create their own dramatic narratives that tie into the social reality of the larger society. They accomplish this by affirming common values and beliefs that will connect them to their audience.

Campaigning is about galvanizing support, so people are motivated to go out and vote for a candidate and support their campaign. This often entails being divisive, negative, and casting the opponent as a villain, so that people will be motivated to vote against them.

Governing is a different process than campaigning. Governing is about unity, creating consensus, and considering the greater good.

Governing is about being gracious, consolatory, and working together with people including those who disagree with you or who are on the opposite side of the political fence.

An incumbent may be tempted to use governing as a means of campaigning by saying that they are doing the people's business as a form of campaigning. As a result, they may be characterized as being aloof and out of touch with the people.

A candidate may be an effective campaigner, but when campaign techniques are used to govern it will carry the divisiveness of the campaign into their administration.

Candidates have different approaches when it comes to campaigning as well as governing, with varying degrees of success.

Campaign like a Democrat, govern like a Republican.

Levels of Political Transformation

Politicians can go through a kind of evolutionary process. They may get stuck in one level, which can inhibit their career. By understanding how this process works, they can make a smooth transitions as their career progresses.

1. The campaigner. When a person enters politics they often capitalize on public discontent with the government. They characterize themselves as an outsider who will change things for the people.

A campaigner gets the people to support them by being divisive, criticizing their opponent, and utilizing conflict to gain support to motivate voters. They use negative campaigning to get people to stop supporting their opponent, so they will support them.

2. The politician. Once in office, a politician has to negotiate with several new groups of people in order to get things done. These can include the other members of an elected body like Congress, as well as with staff, committees, bureaucracy, and their political party.

They will be expected to conform to the rules of these groups in order to receive resources and benefits. This encourages them to go along with them to gain their support. They are now more likely to get things done through compromise and consensus.

3. The leader. In order to advance in government, a politician will have to demonstrate that they are a leader who has leadership qualities. They will have to get the support of others to follow them in order to get things done, which means bringing people together.

4. The statesman. This is a leader who has gained widespread respect and esteem. They put the public's interest above their own political interests. They have experience from years of public service.

They are more concerned with doing what is right than what is politically advantageous. They have the ability to bring people together to get things done. They tend to stay above the political fray by focusing on the big picture.

Chapter 12
The American Version of Social Reality

A clear unified social reality helps society to function effectively. However, it has to change to keep up with changing times. If social reality did not change we would still think that the Sun revolved around the Earth and that the Earth is flat.

Social reality can change in two ways, people change it or events change it for them. Throughout history there have been many pivotal moments that have changed social reality affecting people's behavior like the American Revolution.

It is people's experiences that help provide the basis for sharing meaning to form social reality.

One way social reality changes is through a crisis because people change to adapt to new circumstances. The Great Depression and World War II were crises that motivated people to change their behavior to survive. This affected people for a very long time, creating a social reality of hard work and saving that still exists today.

Social reality would change during the Vietnam War. Instead of uniting society in a single social reality, it would divide society, creating two competing social realities for and against the war.

Many years later this divide has manifested itself in the liberal and conservative divide in society today.

Since then, no one single shared social reality has fully emerged. When there are conflicting social realities there needs to be a release of the tension that is created.

Social reality does not develop overnight. It can take years, perhaps decades for it to manifest itself in physical reality. Social reality has changed in the past, so it will change in the future.

When the existing social reality changes, what will take its place?

Throughout history people have changed their social reality including the structures and institutions of society. Even today, we see different cultures and countries taking very different approaches to how they structure society.

The importance of creating and maintaining social reality extends beyond political campaigns to maintaining the very survival of a nation itself. The creation of a unified social reality has been used throughout history for nation building.

The United States came together as a society with a common social reality of being uniquely American, based on the principles set out by its founders.

As history unfolded, many dramatic narratives are added to the larger American social reality based on their collective shared meanings like the Declaration of Independence, the American Revolution, westward expansion, the Civil War, the Great Depression, World War I and II, and the Cold War, as well as others.

The fracturing of a unified social reality can be seen in other nations like Canada, Spain, and The United Kingdom. These are nations where different social realities manifested themselves in separatist movements, such as Quebec, Scotland, and the Basque region.

In these instances, the nation remained intact, but political concessions often had to be made to keep it together.

In some cases, nations have dissolved like Yugoslavia, Czechoslovakia, and the USSR. In the breakup of the Soviet Union, the people of the former Soviet states such as Latvia, Lithuania, and Estonia did not seem to share a common social reality with Russia, so when given the opportunity, they succeeded from the Soviet Union.

In Germany, unification was possible despite enormous economic and political costs because there is a historically unified social reality.

If America becomes a nation of two or more competing social realities with no unified American social reality, they might find a political voice that can lead to separatist movements that could potentially divide the nation.

Such a division did take place at one time resulting in the Civil War. The lack of any such legitimate political movements signifies that there still is an American social reality, battered though it may be.

However, the increasing polarization of political ideology has become manifested in not only political systems that become increasingly unable to function, but in our communities. This is evidenced by the shrinking number of battleground or swing states and districts in elections.

There is an American social reality to which the public still responds. This does not necessarily include everyone, as within any social reality there may be many views that are shared by different communities, but they tend to support a larger social reality.

This American social reality is demonstrated when the candidates argued over the state of the nation and what should be done about it. No matter how much they disagreed, there is never any criticism of the nation itself or the people.

Candidates may fight over what the government should do, but there is no mention of dismantling the government and starting over. Regardless of political differences, candidates and leaders must support the greater societal social reality for the good of the people and the nation.

When social reality fractures what can be done to restore it? If one version of social reality breaks down, what will take its place? A new social reality can grow naturally from dramatic narratives that share meaning with people throughout society or it can be created intentionally by groups or individuals.

A fractured social reality can be restored to its former state if the people want it. A leader, like the president or presidential candidates can help to forge a social reality that values unity and working together for the good of all people and the nation. It has happened in the past, so it can happen again.

Perhaps the most famous example of changing social reality occurred with the American Revolution.

When the American founding fathers declared independence from Great Britain, they did not march on London or camp out in Trafalgar Square.

They did not go around looting English shops or overturning and burning carriages.

Instead, they prepared a plan to legitimize the new nation and its governmental structure. They formed the Continental Congress and wrote the Bill of Rights, the articles of Confederation, and the Declaration of Independence, which clearly defined their plan for a new nation.

Everyone knew what the new nation stood for and what they are going to do reducing uncertainty. They shared meaning about freedom and democracy that people the world over have invested in for themselves and their families. It was so well thought out it created a stable structure that has provided a model for many nations.

The founders created a social reality that was so strong it has endured for over two centuries.